1 0 0 %

C000085284

⟨m⟩

1 0 0 % R O M E

There's so much to experience in Rome; where do you start? Of course you'll want to visit the Colosseum, the Spanish Steps and the Sistine Chapel. But also be sure to do some shopping on Via Veneto, discover ancient Rome at the Foro Romano, sip cappuccino at a sidewalk café, stroll through the old city's little streets, dine in an authentic Italian family restaurant or go dancing at a trendy nightclub. This guide will take you everywhere you want to go in no time at all - sightseeing, shopping, culinary delights and adventure - and easy-to-use maps will show you the way.

100% ROME: EXPLORE THE CITY IN NO TIME!

Contents

100% Easy-to-Use

To make this guidebook easy-to-use, we've divided Rome up into six neighborhoods and provided a detailed map for each of these areas. You can see
where each of the neighborhoods lies in relation to the others on the general
map in the front of the book. The letters Ⓐ to Ⓦ will also let you know
where to find attractions in the suburbs, hotels, and nightclubs, all described
in detail later on in the guidebook.

In the six chapters that follow, you'll find detailed descriptions of what there
is to do in the neighborhood, what the area's main attractions are, and where
you can enjoy good food and drink, go shopping, take a walk, or just be lazy.
All addresses have a number ①, and you'll find these numbers on the map
at the end of each neighborhood's chapter. You can see what sort of address
the number is and also where you can find the description by looking at
its color:

● = sights   ● = shopping
○ = food & drink   ● = nice to do

6 WALKS
Every chapter also has its own walk, and the maps all have a line showing
you the walking route. The walk is described on the page next to the map,
and it will take you past all of the most interesting spots and best places to
visit in the neighborhood. You won't miss a thing. Not only will you see the
most important sights, museums, and parks, but also special little shops,
good places to grab lunch, and fantastic restaurants for dinner. If you don't
feel like sticking to the route, you'll be able to find your way around easily
with the descriptions and detailed maps.

PRICE INDICATION FOR HOTELS AND RESTAURANTS

To give you an idea of hotel and restaurant prices, you'll find an indication next to the address. The hotel prices mentioned are - unless otherwise stated - per double room per night. The restaurant prices are - unless otherwise stated - an indication of the average price of a main course.

THE ITALIAN WAY OF LIFE

When in Rome, be prepared to put certain expectations of efficiency and precision on hold. Relax, go with the flow and don't get worked up about non-existent bus timetables, restaurants opening later than they say or museums closing earlier than they'd led you to believe.

Food is very, very important in Italy, and generally Romans eat later than northern Europeans and North Americans. Most places serve lunch between 1pm and 3pm, while in the evening only the most touristy restaurants get going before eight. The word 'restaurant' itself should not be taken too literally, because there are many different sub-categories of restaurant. An actual '*ristorante*' is quite a posh and pricey affair. A '*trattoria*' or an '*osteria*' is a simple, often family-run, place where you get home cooking and no fancy décor. '*Pizzerias*' are cheap and lively. Italians tend to drink beer rather than wine with their pizza. An '*enoteca*' is a wine bar where you can also enjoy snacks or light meals. When examining your restaurant bill, don't be surprised by an item called '*coperto*' or '*pane*' - this is a cover charge, calculated per person, usually between €1 and €2. On the other hand, you're not expected to leave a tip, unless the service was really good.

Romans tend not to eat big breakfasts, but usually subsist on a cappuccino and a croissant at the local 'bar', which is something between a cafeteria and a café. To do it the Roman way, pay first at the cash desk and get your receipt, then take it - with a small coin for the guy behind the bar - to the counter, place your order and knock back your coffee. The whole process takes about two minutes. If you want table service and some time to linger, prices will be much higher.

A word on drinking: although it may seem that Italians drink all day long, alcohol consumption is usually limited to wine with food and a few strategically placed 'medical' drinks. The aperitif before dinner is meant to prepare your stomach for the hardship of digesting a meal. It may be something bubbly - a '*spumante*' - or a mixed drink, such as a campari. After dinner soothe your tired intestines with a digestive, that is a distilled drink such as grappa or a herbal bitter, or perhaps a liqueur.

Shops generally close at lunchtime, typically between 1:30pm and 3pm; in the summer months they might reopen later. Most shops are not open on Sundays and Monday mornings. Museums tend to close their ticket offices about one hour before the final closing time, which is what we've given in this guide.

PUBLIC HOLIDAYS

August is the main vacationing month in Italy, and most shops and restaurants in Rome are '*chiuso per ferie*' or closed for the holiday. In addition to Easter Monday, Italians observe the following public holidays:

1 January	- New Year's Day
6 January	- Epiphany 'La Befana'
25 April	- Liberation Day
1 May	- Labor Day
2 June	- National Day 'Festa della Repubblica'
29 June	- Saints Peter and Paul (Rome holiday)
15 August	- Ascension Day
1 November	- All Saints' Day 'I Morti'
8 December	- Immaculate Conception
25 December	- Christmas Day
26 December	- Boxing Day

DO YOU HAVE A TIP FOR US?

We've tried to compile this guide with the utmost care. However, the selection of shops and restaurants can change quite frequently in Rome. Should you no longer be able to find a certain address or have other comments or tips for us concerning this guide, please let us know. You'll find our address in the back of the book.

PALAZZO BARBERINI

Hotels

In the center of Rome there are countless small, family-owned hotels as well as many historic and luxurious upmarket establishments. Generally, big-name chain hotels are near the airport and in other peripheral areas. You can find the letters on the overview map in the front of the book

Some of the smaller hotels are a bit haphazard and disorganized, but they certainly have character and are often in great locations. There are numerous cheap hotels around the central station also, but these are neither charming nor welcoming and you'll get more of a Rome experience if you stay in one of the low-budget places mentioned below.

At the famous, swanky luxury hotels of Via Veneto you'll be rubbing shoulders with celebrities and royalty, but you might have to re-mortgage your house to do so. You can always console yourself with a drink or meal on one of their roof terraces, or a splurge in one of their beauty centers.

Cheap and cheerful - up to €100

(A) **Hotel Parlamento**, as the name suggests, is both close to the parliament building and popular with politicians. It's really excellent value for money considering the central location and the pretty roof terrace, where you can also have breakfast. Air-conditioned rooms - a rare amenity in budget hotels - are available for an extra €11 per day if you make the request when you book. *via delle convertite 5, telephone 066 992 1000, www.hotelparlamento.it, price from €90, bus piazza s. silvestro*

(B) Somewhere to rest your weary head - and not a stroke more! That's the gist of **Pensione Panda**, but what more do you need when you're just around the corner from the Spanish Steps? The rooms are simple and breakfast is not included. *via della croce 35, telephone 066 780 179, www.hotelpandaparadise.com, price from €68, metro spagna*

(c) The basic, brilliantly-located **Hotel Sole al Biscione** has been a lifesaver for budget travelers for decades. Right behind the lively Campo de' Fiori, the rambling old palazzo has rooms for one to four occupants and boasts inviting terraces. There are no breakfast facilities and the hotel doesn't accept credit cards.

via del biscione 76, telephone 066 880 6873 or 066 879 446, www.soleal-biscione.it, price from €95, bus largo di torre argentina

Modest but inviting - €100 to €250

(d) The cordial and professional staff at **Hotel Modigliani** will make you feel at home in no time. Decorated with photographs by the owner, a former children's book author and screenplay writer, there are a few rooms with panoramic views of the city and discounts are available for on-line bookings. The location is perfect: near the nice shops and street cafés of posh Via Veneto and just a short walk from the peaceful Villa Borghese park.

via della purificazione 42, telephone 064 381 5226 or 064 202 7931, www.hotelmodigliani.com, price from €198, metro barberini

(e) **Hotel Locarno** opened in the 1920s and retains much of its original furnishings - you really feel you've entered another era when you come in here. The normal rooms are elegantly decorated and welcoming, but the luxury rooms in the annex across the courtyard are decked out in plush antiques. Extra bonuses include very professional staff and free bicycle rental.

via della penna 22, telephone 063 610 841, www.hotellocarno.com, price from €190, metro flaminio

(f) In a quiet street just north of Piazza Navona, **Hotel Due Torri** has a great location in a quarter that tourists might not usually pass through. The 26 rooms have all been recently restored.

vicolo del leonetto 23, telephone 066 880 6956 or 066 876 983, www.hotelduetorriroma.com, price from €170, bus lungotevere marzio

(G) **Hotel S. Maria** is a real oasis of peace and quiet, right in the heart of the buzzing nightlife of Trastevere. A former convent, the hotel centers on a shady courtyard around which the rooms are arranged. The staff is very professional and helpful and manager Stefano Doghi can also take you on a guided tour of the city.

vicolo del piede 2, telephone 065 894 626, www.htlsantamaria.com, price from €145, tram viale trastevere

(H) **Hotel Farnese** occupies an elegant villa in Prati, a quiet neighborhood near the Vatican that is very good for shopping and public transportation. It's luxurious but discreetly so, with a marble-decorated lobby and cool linen sheets on the beds. From the roof terrace there is a great view of the dome of St. Peter's basilica.

via a. farnese 30, telephone 063 212 553 or 063 211 953, www.hotelfarnese.com, price from €196, metro lepanto

Hey big spender - over €250

(I) The hottest new addition to Rome's tourist accommodation, **es.hotel** decided to go for modern design in an up-and-coming part of town (near the central train station) rather than the antiques-and-tapestries look of the city's traditional hotels. Don't let that fool you into thinking it's not in the same league as the pleasure palaces on Via Veneto - this is five-star rated luxury! The rooms are all unique and designed with modern, minimalist furniture, there is a rooftop swimming pool and spa center and a beautiful panoramic bar and restaurant.

via f. turati 171, telephone 064 448 41, www.eshotel.it, price from €520, metro termini

(J) Behind this romantic, wisteria-covered façade just around the corner from Piazza Navona is **Hotel Raphael**. In this hotel every detail counts, from the Picasso-hung lobby to the individually decorated rooms and charming roof terrace. This is a favorite with discerning bon vivants who shun the flashiness of Via Veneto.

largo febbo 2, telephone 066 828 31, www.raphaelhotel.com, price from €420, bus corso rinascimento

(K) Just off Via Veneto, **Hotel Eden** is over 100 years old, but doesn't show its age at all. It's got the special quality of being welcoming and homey as well as entirely luxurious. The chef at the Michelin-star restaurant La Terrazza dell'Eden used to cook for Prince Charles and Princess Diana at St. James' Palace, and there is a breathtaking view from the rooftop haven of peace. *via ludovisi 49, telephone 064 781 21, www.hotel-eden.it, price from €615, metro barberini*

Transportation

A taxi from Rome's main **airport**, Leonardo da Vinci (Fiumicino), takes about 30 minutes and cost between €40 and €50. There are many unofficial 'taxis' at the airport just waiting to rip off the unsuspecting tourists; only get into a licensed cab. The train ride to Rome's central station with the 'Leonardo Express' costs €8.80 and takes about 40 minutes. If you arrive at Ciampino airport, where the low-cost airlines fly, you're better off using the airline's coach to the center of town, since public transport is complicated. Taxis cost about €40 to €50.

Rome's **metro** system is extremely easy to use: there are only two lines, which cross at Termini station and cover the main sights. The **bus** network reaches the parts of town that the metro doesn't, but be warned that buses can be very crowded and full of pickpockets. To avoid this unpleasant experience, stick to the express buses, which make fewer stops and are less complicated. Between the metro and express bus lines 30 and 40 you'll have most of the center of Rome covered. There are a few **tram** lines, mainly in the suburbs, but lines 8 to Trastevere and line 2 from Piazza del Popolo are useful. Tickets for metro, buses and trams cost €0.77 and are valid for 75 minutes; you have to stamp them on the vehicle to validate them. You can buy tickets at tobacconists and some newsagents, as well as at the main metro stations. There are also one-day, three-day and weekly tickets. If you plan to go out late at night you will find the night buses useful. These connect Rome's most important areas for nightlife between midnight and 5am, and you can buy tickets on board. For information see *www.atac.roma.it*

Taxis are not supposed to stop in the street but should wait for customers at designated taxi stands. Make sure the driver turns on the meter. There are extra charges for luggage, after 10pm and on Sundays and holidays. Tips are not expected. You can call a cab on 063 570.

Rome is a small city, and to make the most of your visit and avoid annoying hassle, the best form of transport is your **feet**. Watch out for crazy traffic, don't take pedestrian crossings too seriously and take your cue from the Romans.

If you're feeling brave, why not do it like the Romans and rent a '**motorino**'? You don't need a license but you do have to wear a helmet. A day out on a moped will set you back about €30. Roma Scooter Rent has two locations, one in Via Paola 12-13 (on the Tiber-end of Corso Vittorio Emanuele II), tel. 066 833 469, and the other in Via in Lucina 13-14 (near the Parliament), tel. 066 876 455. Otherwise try Treno & Scooter in Piazza del Cinquecento, just in front of the main train station Termini, tel. 064 890 5823.

Via Veneto, Trevi Fountain & Pantheon

Via Veneto is the ideal place to experience the high life. This is a side of Rome no visitor (especially those nostalgic for the 60s) would want to miss. The elegant sidewalk cafés and luxury hotels on this tree-lined boulevard will make you hope you win the lottery very soon. This is also a good area for celebrity spotting, as movie stars and royalty tend to stay here when in Rome. Peek into the Galleria Nazionale d'Arte Antica in Palazzo Barberini (it's not just for art buffs). The private apartments are an insight into the lifestyle of the powerful papal Barberini family - an opulent life of excess.

Legend has it that if you throw a coin into the Trevi fountain you'll return to Rome one day. You might not believe it, but are you willing to take the risk? Although this is a great place to cool off during the day, it's also wonderfully romantic at night, when the fountain is lit up.

1

(11)

The area around the Pantheon, Rome's best-preserved ancient monument, is packed with genuine Roman restaurants and small artisan shops. At night, the bars in front of the Pantheon and in Piazza delle Coppelle are great for a drink. The best way to explore this area is just to get lost in the narrow, winding streets, preferably with a delicious ice cream in hand.

6 Musts!

Doney's

Enjoy a cappuccino
at Doney's.

Trevi Fountain

Throw a coin into the
Trevi Fountain.

Quirinale

Admire the view from
the Quirinale.

Pantheon

Look at the sky through
the hole in the Pantheon.

Gelateria della Palma

Get an ice cream at
Gelateria della Palma.

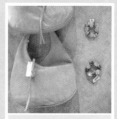

Art'è

Shop for Alessi gear
from Art'è.

○ Sights
○ Shopping

● Food & drink
● Nice to do

Sights

(1) The white Travertine arch in the middle of **Porta Pinciana** has been standing there since the 5th century. If you go through it and look at the gate from the outside, you can see the round, crenellated watchtowers. Worried about Barbarian invaders, Emperor Aurelian, who ruled in the 3rd century AD, had the entire city center ringed with six-meter high walls with watchtowers every 30 meters. To find out more about the walls, visit the Museo delle Mura di Roma at Porta S. Sebastiano, the gate that leads onto Via Appia Antica in the southeast of Rome (see page 139).

porta pinciana, metro spagna, bus via veneto

(2) **Via Veneto** was the backdrop for the 'la dolce vita' lifestyle immortalized in Federico Fellini's film by that name: beautiful people, smart sidewalk cafes, luxury hotels and snap-happy paparazzi. Soak up the atmosphere and peek into the lobbies of the luxury hotels… if you can get past the doormen.

via veneto, metro spagna, bus via veneto

(5) The inconspicuous façade of **S. Maria della Concezione** hides a chilling sight: in the crypt, the bones of over 4,000 Capuchin monks decorate the walls and ceilings of five chapels. Some bones are arranged into Christian symbols, while whole skeletons, including that of a young Barberini princess, are dressed in monks' robes or suspended from the ceiling. The purpose of these horrors is to remind us of our own mortality, with the cheerful message: 'We were once as you are now, you will be as we are'.

via veneto 27, telephone 064 871 185, open daily 9am-noon, 3pm-6pm, admission free, donations requested, metro barberini

(7) **Piazza Barberini** centers on the fountain of the Triton, which sculptor Bernini created for a Barberini pope in 1642. The king of the sea kneels in a shell carried by acrobatic dolphins blowing a jet of water from a conch shell high into the sky.

piazza barberini, metro barberini

(9) **Palazzo Barberini** was built in the 1700s as a residence for the power-ful Barberini family, whose members included the pope of that era. At that time, this area was barely part of the city and the palace was built as a luxu-rious country villa. You might recognise the bees that decorate the doorwa-ys and fountains - they are the Barberini coat of arms and can be seen on monuments all over Rome. The palace houses the Galleria Nazionale d'Arte Antica, which has paintings from the 13th to the 16th centuries, including Raffaelo's famous Fornarina, the recently-restored portrait of the baker's daughter whom he loved.

via delle quattro fontane 13, telephone 06 481 4591, www.galleriaborghese.it, open tue-thu, sun 8.30am-7.30pm, fri-sat 8.30am-10pm, admission €6, metro barberini

(10) The summit of Via delle Quattro Fontane is marked by **le Quattro Fontane** (four fountains) representing the rivers Tiber and Arno and the deities Diana and Juno. The church of S. Carlo alle Quattro Fontane, on which Borromini worked for 29 years, is also here. There is a clear view to the obelisk at the top of the Spanish Steps on one side and the church of S. Maria Maggiore on the other.

via delle quattro fontane, metro barberini

(12) **S. Andrea al Quirinale** is a quirky round church, popular for weddings. It's considered one of the masterpieces of Baroque construction and was designed by Gian Lorenzo Bernini.

via del quirinale 29, telephone 064 890 3187, open wed-mon 8am-noon, 4pm-6pm, metro barberini

(13) From **Piazza del Quirinale** there is a fantastic view of Rome, especially of St. Peter's dome, because (at 61 meters) this is the highest of Rome's seven hills. Take a closer look at the fountain in the square: it's a mixed-up composition with five-meter tall ancient Roman statues, a genuine Egyptian obelisk and a medieval basin that used to be a drinking trough. Palazzo del Quirinale was built as a summer residence for the pope in the 16th century; for a while it was the royal palace for the kings of Italy and since 1947, the presidents of the Italian republic have lived here.

piazza del quirinale, telephone 064 699 2568, www.quirinale.it, palace open sun 8.30am-12.30m (changing of the guard mon-sat 3.10pm, sun 6pm sum-mer, 4pm winter), closed july & august, admission €5, metro barberini

(16) The **Trevi fountain** may be the most famous fountain in the world. In Roman times, legionnaires drank from the water before leaving the city, hoping this would ensure their safe return. These days the tradition is to throw a coin. Standing with your back to the fountain, toss it with your right hand over your left shoulder.

piazza di trevi, metro barberini, bus piazza venezia

(18) A good example of architectural recycling can be seen in **Piazza di Pietra**, where the façade of the stock exchange is the wall of a temple dedicated to emperor Hadrian. A model of the complete temple can be seen in the window of number 36, on the other side of the square.

piazza di pietra, bus largo di torre argentina, piazza venezia

25 **S. MARIA SOPRA MINERVA**

(20) **S. Ignazio** is an amazing church, made even more beautiful by the purpose-designed square in which it is set. Inside is a cacophony of rococo decorations in gilt, stucco and marble. Don't be fooled by the crowning 'dome' on the ceiling - it's just a very good optical illusion!
via della caravita 8/a, telephone 066 794 406, open daily 7.30am-12.30am, 3pm-7.30pm, admission free, bus piazza venezia

(21) The vast, rambling **Palazzo Doria Pamphilj** is actually still inhabited by some of that aristocratic family's descendants. Inside, you can visit the Galleria Doria Pamphilj, an important private collection that includes paintings by Velázquez, Caravaggio and Titian.
piazza del collegio romano 2, telephone 066 797 323, www.doriapamphilj.it, open mon-wed, fri-sun 10am-5pm, admission €7.30, bus piazza venezia

(24) In the middle of **Piazza della Minerva** stands a sculpture of an elephant, bearing an Egyptian obelisk and symbolizing the foundations of wisdom in Christian principles. This sculpture by Bernini is affectionately known as 'Minerva's chick'. Despite the similarity, there's no relationship to Walt Disney's Dumbo.
piazza della minerva, bus largo di torre argentina

(25) Rome's only significant gothic church, **S. Maria sopra Minerva**, was home to Dominican monks who were so unpopular for their religious zeal that they were renamed 'Domini canes', the dogs of the lord. In fact, it was in the convent next to this church that the Inquisition 'questioned' Galileo in 1633 until he took back his belief in the Copernican system. Inside the church are a number of significant works, including Michelangelo's sculpture, Christ Risen, to the left of the altar and frescoes by Filippino Lippo. This is also the final resting place of S. Caterina of Siena (except for her head, which is in a church in her hometown), Fra Angelico and several Medici popes.
via beato angelico 35, telephone 066 793 926, www.basilicaminerva.it, open daily 8am-7pm, admission free, bus largo di torre argentina

(27) Everything about the **Pantheon** is impressive. First built in 27 BC, this newer version is from 118 AD. It became a church in the 7th century. The dome is perfectly proportioned, 43.3 meters across and exactly the same height floor to ceiling. The walls of the building are six meters thick. It was the first ever poured cement ceiling, and it still stands nearly 2,000 years later. The only source of light is from the 'eye' at the top, which really is open to the sky. There are drains in the coloured marble floors, true to the original Roman design, for when it rains. It's not surprising that Raffaelo chose to be buried in this amazing temple rather than in St. Peter's.
piazza della rotonda, open mon-sat 8.30am-7.30am, sun 9am-6pm, holidays 9am-1pm, admission free, bus largo di torre argentina

(34) **S. Luigi dei Francesi** is the French church in Rome. It's most famous for the three Caravaggio paintings (fifth chapel on the left), which depict scenes from the life of St. Matthew. The realistic style of Caravaggio admired today was shocking back then; in fact, his first version of 'St. Matthew with the Angel', depicting a grubby old man and a rather lusty angel, was rejected by his sponsors.
piazza s. luigi dei francesi 5, telephone 066 88 271, open mon-wed, fri-sun 7.30am-12.30am, 3.30pm-7pm, thu 7.30am-12.30am, admission free, bus corso rinascimento

(35) You might notice the security and fancy cars outside **Palazzo Madama** - this has been the seat of the upper house of parliament, the Senate, since 1871. It was the residence of members of the Medici family in the 1500s but the nationalistic decorations inside are much more recent.
corso del rinascimento, www.parlamento.it, open 1st sat of the month 10am-6pm, admission free, bus corso rinascimento

(36) **S. Ivo alla Sapienza** is considered by some to be the culmination of Francesco Borromini's work and it's certainly one of the most cheerful examples of Roman baroque architecture. The crowning spiral lantern on top of the church's dome is instantly recognisable in Rome's skyline. Palazzo alla Sapienza was the seat of Rome's main university until 1935 - it would be difficult to imagine today's 142,000 or so students in there now!
corso del rinascimento 40, telephone 066 864 987, open sun 9am-noon, bus corso rinascimento

Food & drink

(3) To experience a bit of 1960s glamour, treat yourself to a cappuccino at **Doney's**, which together with the Hotel Excelsior takes up almost an entire block between Via Sicilia and Via Boncompagni. The sidewalk café is pure nostalgia, while the lounge and restaurant inside are more modern. Looking up you'll see the Excelsior's famous dome; the suite underneath it covers two floors; a total of 11,700 square feet!
via veneto 141, telephone 064 708 2805, open daily 8am-1am, price €20, metro barberini

(8) The Hotel Bernini Bristol's **L'Olimpo** roof garden restaurant is famous for its 360 degree-view of Rome. What better way to get your bearings of the Eternal City than by picking out famous monuments from this luxurious vantage point? The Sunday jazz brunch here is legendary.
piazza barberini 23, telephone 064 201 0469, www.berninibristol.com, open daily 12.15am-3pm, 7pm-11pm, price €21, brunch €35, metro barberini

(15) **Nonna Papera** (grandma duck) specialises in bruschetta, thickly sliced toasted bread with different toppings, ranging from simple garlic and tomato slices to chilli beans. Not quite a pizza but better than a sandwich, this is a good lunch solution.
vicolo dei modelli 60, telephone 066 783 510, open tue-sun noon-3pm, 7pm-10pm, price €8, metro barberini

(17) The **News Café** is a good place to grab lunch (they make great salads), have an aperitif, or just chill out with a newspaper, which they provide.
via della stamperia 72, telephone 066 992 3473, open mon-thurs 7am-11pm, fri-sat 7am-1am, sun 10am-midnight, price €6, metro barberini

(19) **Osteria del Ingegno** is a popular restaurant with a good wine list and bar. The cozy interior is especially inviting on winter evenings, while the upstairs tables under the arched windows are good to catch the sun. Try the excellent homemade pasta dishes.
piazza di pietra 45, telephone 06 6780 662 or 066 787 481, open mon-sat 12.30am-3pm, 7.30pm-midnight, price €8.50, bus piazza venezia

(28) Revive your spirits with an aromatic espresso at **La Tazza d'Oro**, which imports, roasts and grinds its own coffee - and you can taste the difference. Don't worry if you think you'll never enjoy another cup of coffee again; you can buy some of their special blends to take home. In the summer enjoy a delicious, but very strong, coffee ice (granita).
via degli orfani 84, telephone 066 789 792 or 066 792 768, open mon-sat 7am-8pm, bus largo di torre argentina

(30) Don't be confused by the endless rows of ice cream flavours (chocolate alone comes in 20 variations) at **Gelateria della Palma** - the easiest solution is just to try them all! Look out for the bouquet-like arrangements of sweets and the giant lollipops in the window.
via della maddalena 20-23, telephone 066 880 6752, open daily 8am-1am, bus largo di torre argentina

(31) **Maccheroni** is an established favorite with local celebrities, who like it for its buzzing atmosphere and traditional Roman dishes. Never mind the star gazing though, it's worth coming just for the pumpkin-flower ravioli, which are divine.
piazza delle coppelle 45, telephone 066 830 7895, open daily 1pm-3pm, 8pm-midnight, price €11, bus largo di torre argentina

④ **LIBRERIA LA STRADA**

Shopping

(4) Take a moment to browse through the books at the **Libreria La Strada**. Guidebooks, coffee table photo books and cookbooks spill out into the glass gazebo on the sidewalk. This is a great spot for late-night bookworms.
via veneto 42, telephone 064 824 151, open mon-fri 9.30am-midnight, sat 9.30am-1am, sun 9.30am-1.30pm, 5pm-midnight, metro barberini

(6) **Roux** is a stylish little boutique laden with all the latest accessories and footwear as well as leather jackets and handbags. If your idea of an Italian souvenir is a pair of shoes, then be sure to stop by.
via veneto 6, telephone 064 881 533, open mon-sat 10am-7.30pm, metro barberini

(22) The chocolate shop **Moriondo e Gariglio** was founded in 1886 by two master chocolate makers from Turin, Italy's cocoa capital. The store has a vast array of chocolates, from milk to bitter (up to 80% cocoa!) and beautiful candied and marzipan fruit. For that extra-special surprise for your loved ones at Easter, they'll put surprises of your choice into a chocolate egg.
via di pie' di marmo 21-22, telephone 066 990 856, open mon-sat 10am-7pm, bus largo di torre argentina

(23) The artistic threesome at **coloriage artigianerie** paint their cheerful, colorful designs on anything and everything, including glass, ceramics, mirrors, paper and cloth. The notebooks, photo albums, address books and miniature paintings make great gifts.
via di pie' di marmo 30, telephone 066 919 248, open mon-sat 10.30am-7.30pm, bus largo di torre argentina

(26) **Sciunnach** is the place to stock up on good quality Italian ties. The selection ranges from classic silk to more unusual wool and cotton models. Prices start at €20 for silk and go up to €76 for limited edition woollen ones. For the more adventurous gentleman, there are also unique, hand-painted models with quirky, abstract designs.
piazza della minerva 75, telephone 066 892 922, open mon-fri, sun 9am-7.30pm, bus largo di torre argentina

㉙ **Il Papiro** has excellent quality paper products made in 19th-century Florentine style. Journals and scrapbooks with satisfyingly heavy pages are bound in marbled paper or leather, and souvenir greeting cards and book-marks are decorated with Italian monuments. The boxes and desk sets make good presents, as do the special notebooks: for wine notes, recipes, restaurants, and even old-fashioned hostess books.
via del pantheon 50, telephone 066 795 597,open daily 10am-8pm, bus largo di torre argentina

㉜ If you're tired of the usual techni-colored postcards, try **L'Image** for interesting sketches of artists' impressions of Rome. The selection of posters should also cover most of the paintings you're likely to see in Rome's museums, and the store also carries interesting architectural drawings of churches and monuments.
via della scrofa 67, telephone 066 864 050, open mon-sat 10am-8pm, sun 11am-2pm, 4pm-8pm, bus largo di torre argentina

㉝ Bring home a little piece of Italy from **Art'è**, which stocks the latest in stylish and wacky accessories for the home by well-known designers such as Alessi and Guzzanti.
piazza rondanini 32, telephone 066 833 907, open mon 3.30pm-7.30pm, tue-sat 9.30am-7.30pm, bus largo di torre argentina

Nice to do

(11) The **gardens** along Via del Quirinale are a pleasant oasis on a sunny day; they're small and shady and are probably the closest you'll get to seeing the actual Giardini del Quirinale, the 16th-century gardens of the Quirinale, which are only open once a year on 2 June, the Italian national day.
via del quirinale, open daily sunrise-sunset, admission free, metro barberini

(14) Fun for kids and carbohydrate junkies, the **Museo Nazionale delle Paste Alimentari**, or pasta museum, is the place to learn anything and everything about this popular food, tracing its history from Etruscan times to the present day.
piazza scanderberg 117, telephone 06 699 1119, www.pastainmuseum.com, open daily 9.30am-5.30pm, closed national holidays, admission €9, metro barberini

Via Veneto, Trevi Fountain & Pantheon

Follow the underground walkway from Spagna metro station to Via Veneto - it isn't very well signposted until after the underground car park; or get a bus to the top of Via Veneto ①. Walk down Via Veneto ② ③ ⑥, cross after Libreria La Strada ④ to S. Maria della Concezione ⑤, then go on to Piazza Barberini ⑦ ⑧. At the far end of the square, Via delle Quattro Fontane leads uphill to the entrance of ⑨. Keep going up to the crossing where the four fountains ⑩ are, then turn right and follow Via del Quirinale ⑪ ⑫ to Piazza del Quirinale ⑬. Descend the steps at the far end of the square, follow the street and take the first right into Vicolo Scanderberg, which leads onto Piazza Scanderberg ⑭. With your back to the museum take the small street straight ahead, Vicolo dei Modelli ⑮. Take the next right and you'll suddenly find yourself in front of the Trevi fountain ⑯. If you're hungry, take the street to the right of the fountain to the News Café ⑰. If not, turn left into Via delle Muratte, which takes you across busy Via del Corso (watch out for pickpockets here). Keep going into Piazza di Pietra ⑱ ⑲. Take the first left to S. Ignazio ⑳. Take the street on the right of the church; on the far side of Piazza del Colleggio Romano is Palazzo Doria Pamphilj ㉑. Turn right into Via Pie' di Marmo ㉒ ㉓, keep walking until you come onto Piazza della Minerva ㉔ ㉕ ㉖. You can already see the back of the Pantheon ㉗ from here; walk along Via della Minerva to the front. With your back to the Pantheon, walk straight up past the fountain and you can see La Tazza d'Oro ㉘ just off the square to your right. Go straight into Via del Pantheon ㉙. At the top of the square on the left-hand side is Gelateria della Palma ㉚. Turn left just before it into Via delle Coppelle through Piazza delle Coppelle ㉛ and into Via della Scrofa ㉜. Turn left and you'll come onto Piazza Rondanini ㉝. Also on Via della Scrofa is S. Luigi dei Francesi ㉞. The street to the left comes out on Corso Rinascimento. Turn left past Palazzo Madama ㉟ to Palazzo della Sapienza, cross the courtyard to get to S. Ivo alla Sapienza ㊱.

1. Porta Pinciana
2. Via Veneto
3. Doney's
4. Libreria La Strada
5. S. Maria della Concezione
6. Roux
7. Piazza Barberini
8. L'Olimpo
9. Palazzo Barberini
10. Le Quattro Fontane
11. gardens along Via del Quirinale
12. S. Andrea al Quirinale
13. Piazza del Quirinale
14. Museo Nazionale delle Paste Alimentari
15. Nonna Papera
16. Trevi fountain
17. News Café
18. Piazza di Pietra
19. Osteria del Ingegno
20. S. Ignazio
21. Palazzo Doria Pamphilj
22. Morandi e Gariglio
23. coloriage artigianerie
24. Piazza della Minerva
25. S. Maria sopra Minerva
26. Sciunnach
27. Pantheon
28. La Tazza d'Oro
29. Il Papiro
30. Gelateria della Palma
31. Maccheroni
32. L'Image
33. Art'è
34. S. Luigi dei Francesi
35. Palazzo Madama
36. S. Ivo alla Sapienza

Spagna, Villa Borghese & Tridente

Rome's most fashionable addresses are concentrated around Piazza di Spagna. Even if an outfit by Armani or Valentino isn't likely to become reality for you, it's still fun to join the afternoon strollers for some window-shopping. There are plenty of trendy, affordable stores in the area too, especially on Via del Corso, one of Rome's main shopping streets. The Spanish Steps themselves are a favored hangout for people from all walks of life, and always provide excellent people-watching opportunities.

But of course shopping isn't everything! This part of town is also rich in cafés and restaurants, some world famous, others discreet insiders' secrets. In Rome history is never far from everyday life, so there are also important monuments like the Ara Pacis and the Column of Marco Aurelio to look out for.

2

The park of Villa Borghese, which celebrated a century of being open to the public in 2003, is the city center park of Rome. It's a place for lovers' meetings, family excursions, and picnics with friends and it's also the venue of some of the most beautiful museums in Rome, including the national Etruscan museum and the gallery of modern art.

6 Musts!

Spanish Steps

Sit on the Spanish Steps.

Via Condotti

Window shop on Via Condotti.

Villa Borghese

Stroll through Villa Borghese.

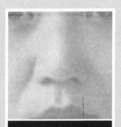

Olfattorio

Do a perfume 'tasting' at Olfattorio.

'Gusto

Treat yourself to a meal at 'Gusto.

Column of Marco Aurelio

'Read' history on the Column of Marco Aurelio.

○ Sights
○ Shopping

● Food & drink
● Nice to do

Sights

① **Piazza di Spagna** takes its name from the Spanish Embassy to the Holy See, which has been on this square since the 17th century. In fact, the area has always been popular with foreigners, as you can see from the many hotels from the 'Grand Tour' era, when a journey around continental Europe was part of every young British aristocrat's education. Probably the most famous staircase in the world, the Spanish Steps were built in the 18th century to connect the French-owned church of Trinità dei Monti at the top to the rest of Rome below. It is one of the city's most popular hangouts, a great place to write postcards, daydream, rest your feet and watch (or experience!) young Italian casanovas at work.
piazza di spagna, www.piazzadispagna.it, metro spagna

② In November 1820, a heartbroken, tuberculosis-ridden poet came to Rome; unfortunately John Keats' stay at the 'Casina Rossa' (the building used to be red) was short. It is now the **Keats-Shelley Memorial House**, and Keats lies buried in the Rome's non-Catholic cemetery along with fellow romantic poet Percy Bysshe Shelley. In the museum are the apartments where Keats died, as well as manuscripts and memorabilia. You can even stay in the upstairs apartment, owned by the British Landmark Trust organization (*www.landmarktrust.co.uk*).
piazza di spagna, telephone 066 784 235, www.keats-shelley-house.org, open mon-fri 9am-1pm, 3pm-6pm, sat 11am-2pm, 3pm-6pm, price €2.80, metro spagna

⑭ Romans have enjoyed the lush, green **Villa Borghese** park since the early 1600s, when it was a powerful cardinal's backyard. It's a great place to wander, have a picnic, roller skate or cycle (bikes are available for hire), row on the lake, go to one of the many museums or to the zoo... you could spend days here! The view from the Pincio, overlooking Piazza del Popolo, should not be missed.
www.villaborghese.it, metro flaminio

⑮ The art collection of the Borghese family in the **Galleria Borghese** is considered one of the leading private collections in the world, even though the debt-ridden Camillo Borghese had to sell over 500 works to his brother-in-law Napoleon; these are now in the Louvre in Paris. Still, the 'leftovers' aren't bad, including work by Raffaelo, Caravaggio, Rubens and Titian. Canova's sculpture of the gorgeous, topless Paoline Borghese (Napoleon's sister) sent her husband into a jealous rage.

piazzale scipione, telephone 06 854 8577, www.galleriaborghese.it, open tue-sat 9am-7pm, sun and holidays 9am-1pm, admission €7.30, booking is obligatory, metro flaminio

(17) This imposing, if somewhat ornate, building houses the **Galleria Nazionale di Arte Moderna**, the national collection of 19th and 20th century art. It covers mostly Italian artists and has an excellent section dedicated to Futurism, a movement from the early 1900s that drew inspiration from industry and the idea of progress. The museum café, with its panoramic terrace, is a lovely place to rest tired feet.

via delle belle arti 131, telephone 063 229 81,
www.gnam.arti.beniculturali.it, open tue-sun 8.30am-7.30pm, admission
€6.50, metro flaminio

(18) Inside this beautiful villa, once a papal summer residence, is the **Museo Etrusco di Villa Giulia**, where you can travel back in time to the 7th century BC to the mysterious world of the Etruscans. This highly sophisticated civilization preceded the Romans in Italy, but very little is known about it. The Etruscans were literate and skilled craftspeople, as can be seen from the remains in the museum, and they strongly influenced the shape of the emerging Roman culture and religion.

piazza di villa giulia 9, telephone 063 201 951, open tue-sun 8.30am-7.15pm,
admission €4, metro flaminio

(19) **Piazza del Popolo** is the tip of the 'Tridente', Neptune's fishing spear, as the three-pronged arrangement of Via di Ripetta, Via del Corso and Via del Babuino is known. It's one of the biggest squares in Rome and is a pleasant place to stroll and look at, with its French-style terraces leading to the Pincio viewpoint above. In pre-airplane, pre-rail times the gate on the north end, Porta del Popolo, was the main entrance to the city. The 25-meter high Egyptian obelisk is from the 13th century BC.

piazza del popolo, metro flaminio

(20) According to popular legend **S. Maria del Popolo** was built on the site of Nero's tomb. Apparently, a walnut tree that grew on the evil emperor's grave was infested with malignant spirits who showed themselves as black crows. An 11th-century pope put an end to this by chopping down the tree and consecrating a church on the spot. The church is decorated with beautiful paintings and sculptures by Raffaelo, Caravaggio and Bernini and also hosts art exhibitions.

piazza del popolo, telephone 063 610 836, open daily 7am-noon, 4pm-7pm,
admission free, metro flaminio

(27) Augustus Caesar, born Octavian, was the first emperor of Rome and the heir of Julius Caesar. The **Mausoleo di Augusto** was intended as a monumental tomb for him and his family, but it takes some creativity to imagine the crumbling, weed-covered ruin in its former state. The building has been used and abused in many ways - it became a fortress in the 12th century and a concert hall in 1908. It took Fascism and Mussolini's brutal determination to resurrect the glories of ancient Rome to clear an area around the tomb and complete its excavation in 1936. The angular white buildings that face the square are from that era.

piazza augusto imperatore, telephone 066 7103 819, visits on appointment, metro spagna

(28) The **Ara Pacis**, or 'peace altar', was constructed between 19 and 9 BC to honor the stability that emperor Augustus had brought to the Roman world - by conquering everything in sight. Marble reliefs depict scenes of battles won and the prosperity of Roman citizens. Some consider them to be the finest marble reliefs ever crafted. But with the fall of the empire, the area was abandoned and the altar was plundered. It took years of excavations and international negotiations to retrieve the pieces, which were finally reassembled under Mussolini. The altar was housed in a protective structure, which was due to be replaced in 2000 with a modern complex by American architect Richard Meier. However, bureaucracy and quibbles have held up the project and the monument is now due to reopen in 2004.

piazza augusto imperatore, no visits at time of writing, metro spagna

(34) The impressive Egyptian obelisk in **Piazza Montecitorio** was brought to Rome by Augustus and served as a sundial nearby. According to some scholars, it was situated so that the shadow would fall on the Ara Pacis on Augustus' birthday. Palazzo Montecitorio is the seat of the lower house of Italian government. The building was started in the 1600s, but was subject to arguments amongst patrons and architects. The latest adjustments were made in the early 1900s when much of the building was redesigned in Italian art nouveau style. Thus, the façade bears no resemblance to what goes on behind it; very apt, considering the ways of Italian politics.

piazza montecitorio, www.camera.it, open first sunday of month 10am-5.30pm, admission free, bus piazza venezia

35 Pause a moment to admire the **Colonna di Marco Aurelio**. The 'cartoon strip' of reliefs depicting the emperor's victories spirals around the column like a parchment scroll. The statue on top was originally of Marcus Aurelius himself, but was replaced by St. Paul in the 16th century. Palazzo Chigi, on the north side of the square, is where the Italian prime minister has his office. *piazza colonna, bus piazza venezia*

Food & drink

(6) You never know who you might rub shoulders with at **Fiaschetteria Beltramme**, a very basic, traditional eatery. It's as popular with local artists and designers as with workers from the street. It's a bit of a tight squeeze, and don't expect haute cuisine or fancy surroundings, but it's lots of fun. Traditional Roman pasta dishes here are excellent.
via della croce 39, telephone none, open mon-sat noon-2pm, 7.30pm-10.30pm, price €10, metro spagna

(9) **Mangiamoci** is a hot new lounge-bar-restaurant and a great place to start or end an evening. While the food is a bit hit or miss - starters and desserts are generally very good, but fancy main courses aim too high - the cocktails are excellent. The squeamish had better sit with their back to the crowded fish tank at the center of the restaurant. The lounge area has low tables and beanbags to chill out on, while a DJ keeps everyone in the mood.
via di s. sebastianello 6/b, telephone 066 780 546, open daily noon-4pm, 6pm-2am, price €12, metro spagna

(11) Art and food blend beautifully in the enduringly popular vegetarian restaurant **Margutta Vegetariano**, whose walls are covered with works by local artists. This is a good place to browse a newspaper over brunch, or to enjoy a fresh, healthy meal.
via margutta 118, telephone 063 265 0577, open daily 12.30pm-3pm, 7.30pm-midnight, price €11, sun brunch €25, metro flaminio

(12) One of the focal points of creativity in this part of town, **Caffè Notegen** has long been a favorite with the artists of nearby Via Margutta. It's the venue of countless exhibitions, book launches and other intellectual events, and it retains a homey, warm atmosphere. The Neapolitan owners, who have been here since 1875, also serve a mean coffee.
via del babuino 159, telephone 063 200 855, open daily 7.30am-1am, price snack €5, metro spagna

(21) **Rosati** hasn't really gone out of style since it opened in the 1920s. The classy, art nouveau café is still the preferred haunt of actors, writers and artists and is an ideal place to round off an afternoon of shopping or sightseeing. *piazza del popolo 4-5/a, telephone 063 225 859, open daily 7.45am-11pm, price drink €6, metro flaminio*

24 A vast selection of wines by the glass awaits you at **Enoteca Buccone**, as well as delicious snacks and light dishes created to go with them. Towering above are shelves upon shelves of bottles, stretching all the way to the vaulted ceilings and groaning under the weight of wine, grappa and liqueurs.
via di ripetta 19-20, telephone 063 612 154, shop open mon-thu 9am-8.30pm, fri-sat 9am-midnight, restaurant open mon-thu 12.30pm-3pm, fri-sat 12.30pm-3pm, 7.30pm-11pm, price €9, metro flaminio

26 **'Gusto** is a perennial favorite with people of all ages and backgrounds because it offers something for everyone. There's a great restaurant with fusion cuisine, a wine bar with live music and an economical pizzeria, plus a pralinerie and a bookshop with about 3,000 food-related books. You might think they're spreading themselves thin with all of this, but actually, 'Gusto is excellent in all its forms. The architecture is stylish without being a slave to fashion. Booking is essential.
piazza augusto imperatore 7, telephone 063 226 273, www.gusto.it, open daily restaurant 12.45pm-3pm, 7.45pm-midnight, pizzeria noon-3pm, 7.30pm-1am, wine bar 11am-2am, bookshop 11am-2am, metro spagna

29 Italians aren't really into breakfast, but **Le Pain Quotidien** is a good place to come for a northern European-style start to the day. Besides a bright, airy atmosphere and fresh-out-of-the-oven bread, tarts and pastries, this café has a picturesque roof terrace where you can also have lunch or brunch.
via tomacelli 24-25, telephone 066 880 7727, open daily 10am-10pm, price €9,50, metro spagna

33 The **Giolitti** family has been making ice cream for over 100 years, marking history with special cups along the way. There's the 'Coppa Olimpica' for the Olympics held in Rome in 1960 and a 'Coppa Mondiali' for the soccer championships in 1990. Choose from over 60 flavors of ice cream or from the patisserie section. There's also a warm lunch buffet on weekdays.
via uffici del vicario 40, telephone 066 991 243, www.giolitti.it, open daily 7am-2am, price ice cream €2.10, bus largo argentina

Shopping

(3) Walking down **Via Condotti** is like leafing through Vogue magazine. Whether you're actually able or willing to buy or wear any of the clothes you see in the windows is irrelevant; it's fun to see what the designers have thought up for the new season. All the big names are represented in Via Condotti or its side streets, from Valentino to Armani, from Gucci to Prada.
via condotti, metro spagna

(4) With all the designer shops around, of course the offspring of the fashion conscious cannot be forgotten. At **Pure** you can find more or less exclusive labels for kids aged 0 to 16, from Dolce & Gabbana Junior and Roberto Cavalli Angels to Blu Marine. The merchandise is organized by age group and the staff is very good at putting together outfits.
via frattina 111, telephone 066 794 555, open mon 1pm-7.30pm, tue-sat 10am-7pm, sun 10.30am-7.30pm, metro spagna

(5) **Galassia** is the place where fashion victims go for a head-to-toe style fix. It stocks the latest trends from Paris, Milan and New York for daring girls who are slim around the waist but fat around the wallet.
via frattina 20-21, telephone 066 797 896, open mon 1pm-7.30pm, tue-sat 10am-7.30pm, metro spagna

(7) The sparkly evening gowns at **Xandrine** are unusual but wearable. There are sequinned dresses and silk skirts in vibrant colors, and accessories (shawls and handbags mostly) to pep up any outfit. If you don't already have an occasion to wear something like this, you'll just have to make one up!
via della croce 88, telephone 066 786 201, open mon-sat 10am-7.30pm, metro spagna

(8) If you find the brightly coloured designs of Alessi's home accessories too shrill, you'll love the subdued tones of **C.U.C.I.N.A.**, where everything is either black, white, chrome or wood. Apart from basic kitchenware, there are also loads of fun and useful gadgets.
via mario de' fiori 56, telephone 066 791 275, www.cucinastore.com, open mon 3.30pm-7.30pm, tue-fri 10am-7.30pm, sat 10.30am-7.30pm, metro spagna

(13) Only the best in lingerie design gets into **Simona**, a shop whose owner is convinced that you can tell a person's cultural refinement by their taste in underwear. There is an enormous selection, from the everyday to the ultra-seductive.
via del corso 82/83, telephone 063 613 742 or 063 600 1836, open mon-sat 9.30am-8pm, metro spagna

(23) Cristina Bomba's style is distinguished by simplicity, natural materials and attention to detail. This goes for everything in her shop, **Bomba**; from knitwear to evening dresses, shoes to jewellery. Chic chicks seek out her smart little handbags. Between her own creations are niches dedicated to other designers who complement her style.
via dell'oca 39, telephone 063 612 881 or 063 203 020, open mon 3.30pm-7.30pm, tue-sat 11am-7.30pm, metro flaminio

(30) **Campo Marzio Penne** is a specialized workshop with both funky modern pens and antique ones, with prices ranging from affordable to ludicrous, but always excellent quality. They can even custom-design pens, and there's a range of relevant accessories, such as leather pen cases, ink, leather-bound notebooks, and brightly colored briefcases.
via campo marzio 41, telephone 066 880 7877, open mon-sat 10am-1pm and 2pm-7pm, metro spagna

(31) What the **Volpetti** family doesn't know about food isn't worth knowing. Whether it's ham, cheese, truffles or wine you're after, the staff in this tasty shop can advise you on finding the best of the best. They also have a pizzeria and cafeteria-style tavola calda where you can get a quick, cheap lunch.
via della scrofa 31/32, telephone 066 861 940 or 066 880 6335, open mon-sat 8am-7pm, sun 9am-8pm, price lunch menu €8, bus largo argentina

(32) **Gioielli in Movimento** is like a toy store for adults. Designer and owner Carlo Cardenà makes unique, transformable pieces of jewellery. There are rings where the stones can be changed, necklaces whose length, shape and style can be altered, and earrings that can be simple studs in the day or dramatic pendants in the evening. All of the jewellery is patented and the all-time favorites are the reversible cufflinks, which can be changed from plain gold to gemstone. At about €500 they're not cheap, but you only live once…
via della stelletta 22/b, telephone 066 867 431, open tue-sat 10.30am-7.30pm, bus largo argentina

Nice to do

⑩ On some Sunday mornings, the artists of the area display their works in the atmospheric **Via Margutta**, where film director Federico Fellini lived for many years.
via margutta, no telephone, market open occasionally, metro spagna

⑯ Elephants, bears, hippos and friends await you in the 12 hectares of parkland that make up Rome's **Bioparco** or zoo, recently redesigned to make it better for animals and visitors. In bad weather, the **Museo di Zoologia** nearby is an attractive alternative.
zoo: piazzale giardino zoologico 1, telephone 063 608 211, www.bioparco.it, open daily 28 oct-29 mar 9.30am-5pm, 30 mar-20 apr, 29 sep-27 oct 9.30am-6pm, 20 apr-28 sep on sat-sun and national holidays 9.30am-7pm, price €8 adults,€6 children, metro flaminio
museum: via ulisse aldovrandi 18, telephone 066 710 9270, www.comune. roma.it/museozoologia, open tue-sun 9am-5pm, price €4.13 adults, €2.58 students, free for children up to 18 years old, metro flaminio

㉒ **Explora Museo dei Bambini di Roma** is a made-to-measure children's world for playing and learning. There's a mini-town with a supermarket, post office and television studio, a play area and a scientific area. Adults are only allowed in if accompanied by a child! Admission is at fixed times for a visit of 1 hour 45 minutes; booking is required.
via flaminia 82, telephone 063 613 776, www.mdbr.it, visits tue-fri 9.30am, 11.30am, 3pm and 5pm, sat, sun and holidays 10am, noon, 3pm and 5pm, price €5 adults, €6 children, metro flaminio

㉕ **Olfattorio** is a 'perfume bar'. You can't buy anything, but you can experience fragrances by sampling the creations of eight French perfumeries in the style of a wine tasting. The helpful staff explains not only the composition of the perfumes you try but also the inspiration behind them, helping you find your scent style. You can then buy your favorite scent from the list of shops they give you.
via di ripetta 34, telephone 063 612 325, open tue-sat 3.30pm-7.30pm, metro flaminio

VIA MARGUTTA ⑩

Spagna, Villa Borghese & Tridente

WALKING TOUR 2

Come out of the Spagna metro station to Piazza di Spagna ① ②, where you won't be able to resist the window shopping in Via Condotti ③, Via Frattina ④ ⑤ ⑥ and Via della Croce ⑦ and around via Mario de' Fiori ⑧ and via di S. Sebastianello ⑨. For more shopping, or a quick bite, walk down arty Via Margutta ⑩ and Via del Babuino ⑪ ⑫ ⑬. Back at the Spanish Steps, walk up the staircase, admire the view and then follow Viale Trinita' dei Monti, past Villa Medici, and up the ramp on the right hand side. Keep going straight to Piazza Napoleone, known as the Pincio. If you want to detour through Villa Borghese park ⑭, take Viale dell'Obelisco, cross the main road, follow Viale delle Magnolie, keep going straight, past the race track, then taking the downhill path on the right until Viale del Museo Borghese ⑮. Following Viale dell'Uccelleria past the flower gardens you get to the zoo ⑯, and you can even glimpse flamingos and monkeys along Viale del Giardino Zoologico. At the end of this road, exit the park to Galleria Nazionale di Arte Moderna ⑰, beyond which lies the Museo Etrusco di Villa Giulia ⑱. Ascend the steps in front of the modern art museum, turn left and go back into the park, past the lake, back onto Viale delle Magnolie and to the Pincio. The steps on the right take you into Piazza del Popolo ⑲ ㉑; to the right of the gate is S. Maria del Popolo ⑳. To get to the Explora Museo dei Bambini ㉒, go through the gate to the tram stop. Heading back into town, take the furthest right of the streets leading off Piazza del Popolo. Via dell'Oca ㉓ is the first on the right. Follow Via di Ripetta ㉔ ㉕ to Piazza Augusto Imperatore ㉖ ㉗ ㉘. With the mausoleum on your right exit the piazza onto Via Tomacelli, cross the road and pass Le Pain Quotidien ㉙ after which turn right into Via del Leoncino. Follow this past Campo Marzio Penne ㉚, and keep going until Piazza del Parliamento, where you turn right into Via dei Prefetti. Keep going until Via della Scrofa, turn left after Volpetti ㉛ into Via della Stelletta ㉜ and keep going straight into Via Uffici del Vicario ㉝ which leads into Piazza Montecitorio ㉞, which in turn leads into Piazza Colonna ㉟.

Foro Romano, Colosseo
Monti & Fori Imperiali

The heart of ancient Rome is an enormous open-air museum. Of course the Colosseo steals the show, but be sure to allow some time to explore the Foro Romano as well. You can wander the ancient streets, sit on fragments of temples, and watch archaeologists as they work. It's amazing to think that these ruins were once the center of an empire. Even if you're not at history expert you can still get a pretty good feel for what it must have been like here 2000 years ago. The Foro comes alive with costumed gladiators and theatrical performances in the summer months.

3

The area around the Foro is notoriously short on good restaurants.
Forget the snack kiosks, whose overpriced offerings are of dubious hygienic
standards. Either pack something to keep you going or head to nearby Monti,
an unspoiled, characteristic part of town where you can have a good bowl of
pasta and enjoy a bit of shopping. Monti is a hotspot for young, up-and-coming
designers and artisans, as you can see from a stroll around Via del Boschetto
and Via dei Serpenti, where new shops keep popping up all the time.

6 Musts!

Vittoriano

Enjoy the view from the café on the Vittoriano.

Foro Romano

Walk along the Foro Romano in the evening.

Gladiator

Pose for photos with the gladiators.

Colosseo

Let the Colosseo take your breath away.

Le Gallinelle

Check out the funky clothes at Le Gallinelle.

Ristorante Forum

Savor a rooftop meal at the Ristorante Forum.

○ **Sights**
○ **Shopping**

○ **Food & drink**
● **Nice to do**

Sights

(1) **Palazzo Venezia** was the embassy of the Republic of Venice in the 16th and 17th centuries. The Museo del Palazzo Venezia houses paintings and decorative arts from that period, including religious art and portraits (check out the ladies' elaborate hairstyles!), tapestries and ceramics. Mussolini used the building as his headquarters; the balcony facing onto Piazza Venezia was the stage for many of his speeches.
via del plebiscito 18, telephone 063 2810, www.ticketeria.it, open tue-sun 8.30am-7.30pm, admission €4, bus piazza venezia

(3) The **Vittoriano**, an enormous, white, nationalistic monument, is not easily missed. Built to commemorate the unification of Italy and to honor Vittorio Emanuele II, the first king of Italy, it houses the tomb of the Unknown Soldier and the altare della patria, the altar of the fatherland. It also incorporates the Museo del Risorgimento, dedicated to the century leading up to Italy's unification. Many Italians consider the structure to be an eyesore, and it's often disparagingly referred to as 'the typewriter' or 'the wedding cake'. You can climb up to the top of the monument for a great view of the city, and hidden around the back (follow the signs to the Caffetteria Ara Coeli) is a nice café that has excellent cakes and desserts.
piazza venezia, telephone 066 991 718, www.quirinale.it, open daily 9.30am-6pm, admission free, bus piazza venezia

(4) It is said that the Romans held the apostle St. Peter captive in the **Mamertine Prison**. He got away by miraculously creating a spring and using the water to baptize his jailers. The prison is now the site of a church and an important destination for pilgrims.
via di s. pietro in carcere, telephone 066 792 902, open daily 9am-12.30pm, 2pm-5pm, donation requested, bus piazza venezia

(6) The **Foro Romano** was the political, commercial and religious heart of Republican Rome. This was where politicians came to hold speeches and attend Senate meetings, where merchants conducted their business, where priests offered sacrifices to the gods, where women did their shopping and where people talked and heard news. As the Roman Empire declined, the Forum fell into neglect and by the 5th century AD it was abandoned. The area became pasture land and was known as the Campo Vaccino or cow field. The majestic marble temples were plundered for building materials or converted for other uses. It was only during the Renaissance that a love for all things classical revived interest in the area and in the 17th century excavations were started.

entrances in via di s. pietro in carcere, in via dei fori imperiali and in piazza venere e roma near the arch of titus, telephone 063 996 7700, www.archeorm.arti.beniculturali.it, open daily 9am-4.30pm, admission free, guided tours in english sat and sun noon, bus piazza venezia, metro colosseo

(7) The **Via Sacra** was the most important road in the center of ancient Rome. Its name comes from the many temples that stood alongside it and it was used for processions of all sorts, most importantly the triumphal procession, which a general could request from the Senate if he had won a war, gained territory, and killed at least 5,000 enemy soldiers. The march would include people acting out battles, enchained prisoners and war booty, soldiers who had fought in the war and finally the leader of the conquered army, who would then be publicly executed.

info as foro romano, www.archeorm.arti.beniculturali.it, bus piazza venezia, metro colosseo

(8) The **Curia** was the meeting place of the Roman Senate. Here, 300 experienced men debated laws and acted as advisors to the two consuls leading the Republic. The Curia was converted into a church in the Middle Ages but in the 1930s it was deconsecrated and restored. Note the high ceilings and the excellent acoustics.

info as foro romano, www.archeorm.arti.beniculturali.it, bus piazza venezia, metro colosseo

(9) When Julius Caesar was murdered in 44 BC, the Roman people could not believe the dictator was dead. The Senate ordered a public cremation and the erection of an honorary altar, the **temple of Divus Iulius**, for all to see. Thirteen years later, Caesar's adopted son Augustus had a temple built over the site and declared Julius a god. The deification of emperors later became common practice.

info as foro romano, www.archeorm.arti.beniculturali.it, bus piazza venezia, metro colosseo

(10) The small, round **temple of Vesta** was extremely important in ancient Rome, as she was the goddess of the hearth and protector of the family. It was thought that if the sacred fire inside the temple went out it would spell disaster for Rome. The duty to tend the eternal flames fell to the Vestal Virgins, six girls who entered the priesthood between 6 and 10 years old and remained in service for 30 years. They lived in the convent-like **house of the Vestal Virgins** behind the temple and enjoyed the highest respect and privileges. However, they were strictly ruled - if they let the sacred fire go out, or if their chastity was doubted, they were buried alive.
info as foro romano, www.archeorm.arti.beniculturali.it, bus piazza venezia, metro colosseo

(11) The **temple of Faustina and Antonino** was built by the Emperor Antoninus Pius in memory of his wife Faustina; when he died the dedication was extended to him as well. It's interesting because a church was built into the temple in the 8th century, using the ancient pillars as a portico. Looking at the door of the church you can see how high up it is. This is the level to which the abandoned Forum was filled with dirt and rubble when it was abandoned.
info as foro romano, www.archeorm.arti.beniculturali.it, bus piazza venezia, metro colosseo

(12) The last and largest of Rome's ancient basilicas, the **Basilica di Massenzio** was started by emperor Maxentius and finished by emperor Constantine in 312 AD. These days, a 'basilica' is a type of church but back then the word referred simply to an indoor meeting place. The building was 100 meters long and 65 meters across, and in the apse on the far end stood a colossal statue of Constantine. (Bits of this, including the 2.6-meter high head, can be seen in the Capitoline Museums, see Chapter 4 (19)). Architecturally the building was amazing, with the ceiling held up by vaults and arches, without any support beams, and reaching the height of 35 meters in the middle - about the height of a ten-story modern building. This roof lasted for over 1,000 years, but collapsed in an earthquake in the 14th century.
info as foro romano, www.archeorm.arti.beniculturali.it, bus piazza venezia, metro colosseo

(13) Legend, supported by archaeological finds, says that Rome's first inhabitants, including Romulus and Remus, lived on the **Palatino** or Palatine hill. In Republican Rome the hill was a residential quarter for well-to-do families, and in Imperial times it became the venue for the grandiose residences of the emperors. The world 'palace' derives from the name of the hill. You can see the remains of the palaces of Augustus, his wife Livia, and many of their successors. There is even a private stadium.

entrance from the roman forum, arco di tito end, telephone 066 990 110, www.archeorm.arti.beniculturali.it, open daily 1 nov-15 feb 9am-4.30pm, 16 feb-15 mar 9am-5pm, 16 mar-31 mar 9am-5.30pm, 1 apr-31 aug 9am-7.30pm, sep 9am-7pm, oct 9am-6.30pm, admission €8 for palatino and colosseo, metro colosseo

(14) The **Arco di Constantino** was erected in 312 AD by order of the Senate, as a triumphal monument to honor emperor Constantine for liberating Rome from the 'tyrant' Maxentius. At this time, however, the Roman Empire was long past its prime, and the best artists had moved east to Constantinople, the new capital. So the triumphal arch was decorated with fragments from the past, ranging from 98 to 180 AD, from the reign of Trajan, Marcus Aurelius and Hadrian. Only the small reliefs that run around the monument actually depict scenes that involved Constantine.

between via di san gregorio and piazza del colosseo, www.archeorm.arti. beniculturali.it, metro colosseo

(15) Though it was known as the Flavian Amphitheatre in its time, today we call it the Colosseum or **Colosseo**. Its inauguration in 80 AD was celebrated with 100 days and nights of games, during which some 5,000 wild animals met their death. All sorts of 'games' were staged here, from gladiator fights to animal hunts, and even naval battles. The Colosseum could hold more than 50,000 spectators. On particularly hot days a special force of marines anchored a huge tarpaulin over the structure to provide the audience with shade. A complex system of underground passages and trap doors allowed gladiators and animals to appear on stage as though out of nowhere.

piazza del colosseo, telephone 063 996 7700, open daily 9am-7.30pm, www.archeorm.arti.beniculturali.it, admission €8 for colosseo and palatino, metro colosseo

(17) The **Domus Aurea** or 'golden house' was the vast palace built by Nero, who became emperor at the age of 17, and who had more than a few screws loose. While Nero's mother poisoned her husband to get Nero to the throne, he repaid her by having her assassinated a few years later. More interested in the arts and pleasure than ruling the empire, he had this enormous palace built after the great fire of 64 AD, which he allegedly watched unmoved, while singing and playing his lyre. The palace took up a quarter of the area of the city as it was then. Nero was eventually declared a public enemy and committed suicide while on the run. The rooms that have recently been opened to the public house some of the most important frescoes of antiquity.

viale della domus aurea, telephone 063 996 7700, www.archeorm.arti.beni-culturali.it, open mon, wed-sun 9am-7.45pm, june-sept also 9pm-11.45pm, admission €5, metro colosseo

(18) The church of **S. Pietro in Vincoli** is special for art-lovers and pilgrims alike. Under the main altar are the chains that bound St. Peter - the story goes that a piece of the chains that held him in Jerusalem fused miracu-lously with a piece of the chains that bound him in Rome (see {4}). The other big highlight is Michelangelo's unfinished tomb of Julius II, featuring the powerful, horned Moses.

piazza di s. pietro in vincoli 4/a, telephone 064 882 865, open mon-sat 7am-12.30pm, 3.30pm-7pm, sun 8.45am-11.45pm, admission free, metro cavour

(29) Mussolini, in a project that was as drastic as any thought up by the Roman emperors, built the Via dell'Impero, now **Via dei Fori Imperiali**, right over the Imperial Fora to connect Piazza Venezia with the Colosseum. The project necessitated the demolition of numerous 16th-century palaces, and archaeo-logists have lost access to nearly half of the remains from imperial Rome. The road is closed to traffic most Sundays.

via dei fori imperiali, bus piazza venezia, metro colosseo

㉚ When Rome became an empire and the city started growing almost as rapidly as its rulers' egos, the Roman Forum was no longer big enough, and the **Fori Imperiali** were built. Julius Caesar was the first to build a new meeting area, and his adoptive son followed suit 50 years later, with the nearby forum of Augustus. At the far end of Via dei Fori Imperiali is the Temple of Peace, which started as a display area for bounty looted in Middle Eastern battles. Emperor Nerva didn't have much room left when his turn came, so his forum is squashed between the Forum of Augustus and the temple. The valley between the Capitoline hill and the Quirinale hill was now full - but that didn't stop the emperor Trajan from building the most grandiose of the imperial complexes: he actually cut back and dug away part of the Quirinale hill to make room for his forum.

via dei fori imperiali, bus piazza venezia, metro colosseo

㉛ The scroll-like relief that winds around the **Colonna di Traiano** depicts the emperor's victories in Dacia, present-day Romania. It was the spoils of this war that financed the construction of his forum. The height of the column marks the height of the hill that was dug away to make room for the forum (see ㉚).

via dei fori imperiali, bus piazza venezia

㉜ The supermarket of ancient Rome, the department store of the emperors - the **Mercati di Traiano** were the one-stop shopping solution of his day. Six floors of shops sold everything from wine and spices to fish (kept alive in tanks), fruit and vegetables. The entrance hall of the markets often hosts temporary exhibitions.

via IV novembre 94, telephone 066 790 048, open tue-sun 9am-6pm, admission €6.20, bus piazza venezia

Food & drink

(19) If a beer might help you recover from a long day of walking around the Roman Forum, **Finnegan's** is the answer. It's a cozy and welcoming Irish pub, with good beer and tables outside in the summer.
via leonina, telephone 064 747 026, open mon-thu noon-00.30am, fri-sat noon-1am, sun 1pm-00.30am, metro cavour

(20) A simple restaurant that is fun, convivial and good value for money: that's what **Vecchia Roma** is all about. It's nothing fancy, but the food is good, especially if you let the exuberant owner advise you. Traditional Roman pasta dishes and unbelievably fresh fish are the specialities.
via leonina 10, telephone 064 745 887, open mon-sat 12.30pm-3pm, 7.30pm-midnight, price €8, metro cavour

(22) The tables in the shady square outside **Osteria degli Angeletti** seem to beckon, telling you to rest your weary feet. The pasta is excellent - be sure to ask what the daily special is.
via dell'angeletto 3, telephone 064 743 374, open daily noon-3pm, 7pm-11.30pm, price €10, metro cavour

(27) Pizza in every imaginable form and variation is what you get at **Al Giubileo**; 70 different types, to be precise, from buffalo mozzarella and cherry tomatoes to nutella. You can try them all (or as many as you can handle) in a special taster menu. The deep-fried 'fritto misto' starter and the homemade desserts are worth saving room for.
via del boschetto, telephone 064 859 29, open daily 7pm-12.30am, price menu €9.80, €7, bus via nazionale, metro cavour

(28) Many hotels in Rome have rooftop terraces, but for a panoramic view of the Foro Romano and the Colosseo, the **Ristorante Forum** at the Hotel Forum is unbeatable. Even if you don't want to fork out the €320 for a double room, you can still stop by for a copious American breakfast, lunch, dinner or sundowner cocktails. The cuisine is Roman and Sardinian, so you can taste interesting seafood and hearty meat dishes.
via tor de' conti 25, telephone 066 792 446, www.hotelforum.com, open daily breakfast 8am-10.30am, lunch 1pm-3pm, dinner 8pm-11pm, price €12, metro colosseo

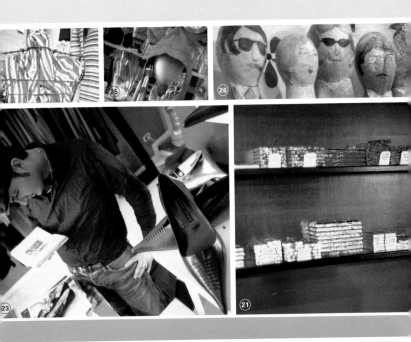

Shopping

(21) How about this for a souvenir: a monument of the Eternal City sculpted in chocolate, from the **Bottega del Cioccolato**. Alongside normal pralines and chocolates, these exquisite artisans make tiny reproductions of the Colosseum and St. Peter's in the purest dark chocolate. Such a souvenir isn't likely to last very long.
via leonina 82, telephone 064 821 473, open mon-fri 9.30am-7.30pm, metro cavour

(23) **Via degli Zingari 10** is one of numerous hip, unusual boutiques that have sprung up in Monti in recent years. The plush, shocking pink interior is intimate and boudoir-like, while the clothes are hand picked from designers in Italy and France. There's also a range of super-chic shoes.
via degli zingari 10, telephone 064 782 3889, open mon 4pm-8pm, tue, fri-sat 10am-8pm, wed-thu 10am-10pm, metro cavour

(24) Colorful, welcoming and relaxed - these words describe **Arcana Celestia**, the clothes inside the shop and the two women in charge.
via del boschetto 127, telephone 0648 23572, open mon-sat 10.30am-8pm, metro cavour

(25) Every time you squeeze into the hole-in-the-wall **Io Sono Autarchico** it's an exploration into uncharted territory. The store is chock-full of home accessories, kitchenware and gadgets, ranging from retro nostalgic 50s tin pots to brightly colored plastic modern designs. The selection changes all the time, so you never know what you might find; excellent for bargain hunters.
via del boschetto 92, telephone 064 844 77, open mon 4pm-8pm, tue-sun 10am-1.30pm, 4pm-8pm, bus via nazionale, metro cavour

(26) Vintage is the name of the game at **Le Gallinelle**, either in the form of selected outfits from the 60s and 70s, or new models made from old fabric that owner, designer and tailor Wilma has dug up somewhere.
via del boschetto 76, telephone 064 881 017, www.legalinelle.it, open mon 4pm-8pm, tue-sun 10am-1pm, 4pm-8pm, bus via nazionale, metro cavour

Nice to do

(2) The **Time Elevator** 'virtual reality' tour takes you through the 3,000 years of history of ancient Rome in a blaze of special effects. Part amusement park ride, part cinema, part sneaky history lesson, it's a good, brief (45 minutes) introduction to a day's wandering through history.
via dei ss. apostoli 20, no telephone, www.time-elevator.it, open daily 9am-midnight, screenings every 15 minutes, admission €11 adults, €9.20 children, bus piazza venezia

(5) **The Miracle Players** put ancient Rome into perspective. This fun group of English-speaking actors recounts the history of Rome and the lives of the most important emperors, all in 40 minutes. Their scripts draw on classical writing but their approach is fun and easily digestible. The performances are in a piazza in front of the forum.
via di s. pietro in carcere (in front of mamertine prison), www.miracleplayers.org, metro colosseo

(16) You can hardly miss the splendid centurions and **gladiators** in full costume hanging out in front of the Colosseum. They are there to pose for photos with you, for a fee. Don't try to photograph them on the sly, as they're likely to come after you with their swords.
piazza del colosseo, price from €3, metro colosseo

Foro Romano, Colosseo
Monti & Fori Imperiali

Take a bus to Piazza Venezia. Facing the monument, Palazzo Venezia ① is on your right, with the entrance in the side street. To get to the Time Elevator ② cinema go up Via del Corso behind you, it's the second on the right. Climb up the Vittoriano ③ and exit through the Museo del Risorgimento, keep going straight and you'll have the church with the Mamertine Prison ④ underneath it on your right ⑤. Go down the stairs on the far end of the square into the Foro Romano ⑥. Follow the Via Sacra ⑦ through the arch, past the Curia ⑧ on your left and to the temple of Divus Iulius ⑨ in the center. Cross to the right of that, going straight until you get to the temple of Vesta ⑩ and on the far left you can see the temple of Faustinia and Anitonius ⑪. Crossing back onto the Via Sacra and heading up to the left you come to the remains of the Basilica di Massenzio ⑫. The entrance to the Palatino ⑬ is to the right of the Arco di Tito; going past the arch down the ramp takes you to the valley of the Colosseum, with Arco di Costantino ⑭ to your right and the Colosseum ⑮ ⑯ straight ahead (hard to miss). Cross the road in front of the metro stop, and take the staircase slightly to the right, turn right at the top and keep going to get to Domus Aurea ⑰ or turn left into Via delle Terme di Tito. At the square at the top take Via Eudossiana to S. Pietro in Vincoli ⑱. The staircase under the low arch takes you to Via Cavour; cross this and descend the staircase on the other side to Via Leonina ⑲ ⑳ ㉑. Turn right on Via dell'Angeletto ㉒, which after Via degli Zingari on your right ㉓ becomes Via del Boschetto ㉔ ㉕ ㉖ ㉗. Cross over to Via dei Serpenti and go past the square, then turn right into Via Madonna dei Monti, at the end of which is the Hotel Forum, with the Ristorante Forum ㉘. Get back on to Via dei Fori Imperiali ㉙ and follow it along the Fori Imperiali ㉚. The Colonna di Traiano ㉛ is at the Piazza Venezia end. A steep staircase behind the column leads to Via IV Novembre and the entrance to the Mercati di Traiano ㉜.

1. Palazzo Venezia
2. Time Elevator
3. Vittoriano
4. Mamertine Prison
5. The Miracle Players
6. Foro Romano
7. Via Sacra
8. Curia
9. Temple of Divus Iulius
10. Temple of Vesta
11. Temple of Faustina and Antonio
12. Basilica di Massenzio
13. Palatino
14. Arco di Costantino
15. Colosseo
16. Gladiators
17. Domus Aurea
18. S. Pietro in Vincoli
19. Finnegan's
20. Vecchia Roma
21. Bottega del Cioccolato
22. Osteria degli Angeletti
23. Via degli Zingari 10
24. Arcana Celestia
25. Io Sono Autarchico
26. Le Gallinelle
27. Al Giubileo
28. Ristorante Forum
29. Via dei Fori Imperiali
30. Fori Imperiali
31. Colonna di Traiano
32. Mercati di Traiano

- ● Sights
- ● Food & drink
- ○ Shopping
- ● Nice to do

- ● Sights
- ● Food & drink
- ○ Shopping
- ● Nice to do

Largo Argentina, Ghetto & Caracalla

The Jewish area of Rome (still called the 'ghetto' by many) is squeezed between the Capitoline hill and the Tiber. It is fun to wander the tiny streets streets and observe the details on every street corner, and to taste the local specialties. The Capitoline hill or Campidoglio was one of the most important places in ancient Rome, and today it's the seat of the mayor's council. Don't miss the fantastic view over the Roman forum from the back of the square. At the Musei Capitolini, with its beautiful Roman sculptures, you can see that the Romans weren't only about war and conquering but also excelled at the arts.

4

Thanks to Hollywood, there are parts of Rome that you feel like you've known all your life. Certainly the Bocca della Verità was immortalized by Audrey Hepburn in 'Roman Holiday', and the Circo Massimo was burned into our brains in 'Ben Hur'.

What do you like best about Rome: is it the quiet gardens and churches, the panoramic views, the remains of an ancient civilization or the great food and hip bars of a buzzing modern city? All of these can be yours, just minutes' walk from one another.

6 Musts!

Cats

Watch the cats at the Largo di Torre Argentina Cat Sanctuary.

Chiesa del Gesù

Admire the ceiling frescoes of the Chiesa del Gesù.

Da Giggetto

Savour the fried artichokes at Da Giggetto.

Isola Tiberina

Sunbathe on the Isola Tiberina.

Spazio Sette

Give in to your gadget buying tendencies at Spazio Sette.

Four XXXX Pub

Chill out at the Four XXXX Pub in hip Testaccio.

○ Sights
○ Shopping

● Food & drink
● Nice to do

Museo Nazionale Romano
Crypta Balbi

ORARIO
TIMETABLE

9-19 (uscita 1...
lunedì chius...
closed on m...

BIGLIETTI
TICKETS

Ingresso	lire 8.000	
Entrance	euro 4.13	
Ingresso ridotto	lire 4.000	
Half price ticket	euro 2.07	
Visita con archeologo		lire 6.000
Guided tour	euro 3.10	
Prenotazione gruppo	lire 50.000	
Group reservation	euro 25.82	
Prenotazione gruppo con archeologo		lire 150.000
Guided tour group reservation	euro 77.46	

... gruppi obbligatoria

...lefono 06 39967700

Sights

(1) The **Area Sacra dell'Argentina**, with its four temples that count as some of the oldest in Rome, was discovered during construction work in the 1920s. A certain amount of secrecy on the part of Mussolini's administration and a primary concern for glorifying the discovery rather than studying it meant that the area was not excavated as fully as it could have been and many questions are still unanswered. Some archaeologists believe that this is where the Curia of Pompeio was - the place where Julius Caesar was murdered.
largo di torre argentina, closed to the public except for guided tours (see torre argentina cat sanctuary, page 93), bus largo di torre argentina

(7) The museum of the **Crypta Balbi** takes you through the history of this part of town, from imperial Roman times, when the theater and crypta of Balbus, an important general, stood here. Parts of the impressive structure were used as squats, baths, kilns, latrines, noble palaces, merchants' shops and in medieval times as a nunnery for the daughters of prostitutes. This is a good introduction to what goes on below the present-day street level in Rome.
via delle botteghe oscure 31, telephone 063 996 7700, www.archeorm.arti.beniculturali.it, open tue-sun 9am-7.45pm, admission €4, bus largo di torre argentina

(8) A new church and a new architectural style for a new religious order, that's the **Chiesa del Gesù**. 'Il Gesù' was built between 1568 and 1584 as the home for the new Jesuit order, a special taskforce of teachers and missionaries. Ignatius of Loyola, the founder of the order who is buried in the left transept, wanted the church to direct the congregation's attention on the main altar. The solution was a cross-shaped floor plan with the altar in front of the top apse, a design that has been replicated in innumerable churches since. The Triumph of the name of Jesus seems to explode through the ceiling from the heavens above.
piazza del gesù, telephone 066 786 341, open daily winter 6am-12.30pm, 4pm-7.15pm, summer 6am-12.30pm, 4pm-7.30pm, bus largo di torre argentina

(9) In the 1500s the Mattei family owned five palaces, each around the corner from the other, causing this area to be called 'Mattei Island'. The turtle fountain in the centre of **Piazza Mattei** is the heart of this island. A popular story recounts that a young nobleman in financial difficulties wanted to prove to the father of his beloved that he was still capable of great things and had the fountain built for her overnight.

piazza mattei, bus largo di torre argentina

⑭ **TEATRO DI MARCELLO**

⑭ You're not seeing double, it's not another Colosseum! The **Teatro di Marcello**, one of the largest theatres of ancient Rome, was started by Julius Caesar and finished by Augustus around 12 AD, but never served for gladiator fights or sports. Augustus dedicated it to his beloved nephew, Marcelus, who died young.

entrances to grounds in via foro piscario (via del portico d'ottavia) and in via del teatro marcello, no telephone, grounds open daily 9am-5pm, bus piazza venezia

⑮ The **Sinagoga** and the **Museo della Comunità Ebraica** are at the heart of the Jewish part of Rome. At 2,000 years, it's the oldest Jewish community in Europe, and has been subjected to persecution, especially in the 16th century when an anti-Semitic pope had them confined to the cramped ghetto area, regulations that were in force for over 200 years. Tragedy returned with Italy's fascist era and the deportations of World War II. The synagogue is under constant military surveillance since a bomb attack in 1983.

lungotevere cenci, telephone 066 8400 661, museum open sep-apr mon-thu 9am-4pm, fri 9am-1.30pm, sun 9am-noon, may-aug mon-thu 9am-7.30pm, fri 9am-1.30pm, sun 9am-noon, admission €6, bus largo di torre argentina

⑯ The peaceful **Isola Tiberina** has been associated with healing since the 3rd century BC, when a temple was erected for a sacred snake that cured the city of the plague. There is a hospital on the island to this day. The bridge from the Ghetto to the island is the original structure from Roman times.

isola tiberina, bus largo di torre argentina

⑱ The world 'capital' derives from Capitolinum, the Latin name for the Campidoglio, which has been an important hill since before Roman times. **Piazza del Campidoglio** as we see it today is based on the designs of Michelangelo, who redesigned in Renaissance style the façades of the existing buildings: the Palazzo Senatorio on the top side and the Palazzo dei Conservatori on the right-hand side. A third building, Palazzo Nuovo, was constructed on the remaining side to give the piazza its trapezoid shape, with the grand staircase on the fourth side leading east towards St. Peter's and so shifting the focus away from the Roman Forum. The equestrian statue in the middle is a computer-generated copy of a second century sculpture of emperor Marcus Aurelius; the original is in the Musei Capitolini.

piazza del campidoglio, bus piazza venezia

(19) The **Musei Capitolini** is the collective name for the museums and galleries in Palazzo dei Conservatori and in Palazzo Nuovo. The collections of classical sculpture came to the city through donations by various Popes, and in 1734 this became the first public museum in the world. In the courtyard of Palazzo dei Conservatori are the famous fragments of the colossal statue of Constantine from the Basilica of Maxentius (see Chapter 3), as well as the Lupa Capitolina, an Etruscan sculpture from 500 BC depicting the she-wolf said to have suckled Romulus and Remus.

piazza del campidoglio, telephone 063 996 7800, www.museicapitolini.it, open tue-sun 10am-8pm, admission €6.20, bus piazza venezia

(20) Two temples are all that remain of the **Foro Boario**, the ancient cattle market. They date from the 1st and 2nd centuries BC, and are so well pre-served because they did time as churches. The round temple was dedicated to Hercules Victor, while the square one (the typical Roman layout with a portico in the front) was for Portunus, god of ports. In fact, one of the major ports of the Tiber was located nearby.

lungotevere dei pierleoni / piazza della bocca della verità, metro circo massimo

(21) The **Bocca della Verità**, the Medusa-like head said to bite off the hand of those who lie, is actually an ancient drain cover. One legend says it was enchanted by a magician to test the virtues of married women… Who knows what the truth is - stick your hand in the mouth and see what happens.

chiesa di s. maria in cosmedin, piazza della bocca della verità, telephone 066 781 419, church open daily 10am-1pm, 3pm-5pm, portico open daily 9am-6pm, metro circo massimo

(22) Chariot racing was to the Romans what soccer is to the Italians, and the **Circo Massimo** is where it all happened. It was immensely popular - the racetrack had seating for over 250,000 spectators - and it commanded fierce team loyalties. Victorious charioteers were the Beckhams of their day, if they survived. Casualties were common since the sport had few rules. The Circo Massimo was one of the most constant features of ancient Rome - the area was used for sports since the 6th century BC, and all of the emperors were keen to add to their popularity by elaborating the complex.

circo massimo, metro circo massimo

25 A politically contentious obelisk if ever there was one, the **Obelisco di Axum** was taken from Ethiopia by Mussolini in 1937 to place in front of what was then the Ministry for Africa, now the headquarters of the United Nations Food and Agriculture Organization. Italian governments have been promising to return the obelisk to its home country since 1947. The latest setback came in May 2002, when lightning shattered the tip of the structure. Archaeologists believe it may now be too delicate to transport.

piazza di porta capena, metro circo massimo

26 The **Terme di Caracalla** weren't just public baths but a luxurious leisure center, one of the most elaborate complexes of their kind. The Romans were into these spa-sports centers, and at one point there were nearly 1,000 of them in the city. At the Baths of Caracalla there were gyms and playing fields, libraries and service areas that could cater for elaborate banquets, saunas and massage rooms, hot, tepid and cold baths and swimming pools. All of the buildings were elaborately decorated with mosaics, paintings and stuccowork. The baths were open to all Roman citizens, and could have held up to 1,600 people.

via delle terme di caracalla, telephone 063 996 7700, www.archeorm.arti.beni-culturali.it, open tue-sun 9am-4.30pm, admission €5, metro circo massimo

27 A **pyramid** in the middle of Rome? You'd better believe it, because at a time when Egypt was part of the empire and Julius was smooching Cleopatra, Egypt-mania was raging through the city. Whether it was Nubian slaves, imported obelisks or worshipping Egyptian gods, everyone was fascinated by that ancient culture. The nobleman Caio Cestio took it one step further by having a pyramid as his funerary monument.

piazzale ostiense, metro piramide

28 The **Cimitero Acattolico**, the non-Catholic cemetery, is the final resting place for no end of celebrity (and normal) foreigners, most famously John Keats and Percy Bysshe Shelley. It's also where Antonio Gramsci, founder of the Italian communist party, is buried. It's a haven of peace and quiet, despite the traffic zooming around outside the walls.

via nicola zabaglia 45, telephone 065 741 900, www.protestantcemetery.it, open oct-mar tue-sun 9am-5pm, apr-sep 9am-6pm, ring the doorbell, admission free, donations welcome, metro piramide

29 The 'hill' of **Monte Testaccio** is actually made of Roman pot shards - it was a dumping ground for the busy warehouses that stood along the river. You can see cross sections of the hill in many of the restaurants that stand at its foot, and there's an exposed bit on the corner of Via Zabaglia and Via Galvani.

metro piramide

Food & drink

(5) Tradition (and Renato) rules the kitchen at **Renato e Luisa**, a welcoming and relaxed restaurant. Prime ingredients go into no-nonsense, generous and carefully prepared recipes. You will never leave here hungry, unsatisfied or too far out of pocket.
via dei barbieri 25, telephone 066 869 660, open tue-fri 12.30pm-3pm, 8.30pm-midnight, sat-sun 8pm-midnight, price €9, bus largo di torre argentina

(6) **Le Bain** has a reputation for going out of its way to find the best possible products. Cheeses, salami and oil are all made by small artisan producers. If this quality is reflected in the prices, then at least you know where your money is going. The Sunday champagne brunch is a welcome treat.
via delle botteghe oscure 32/a-33, telephone 066 865 673, open tue-sat 7pm-2am, sun noon-3pm, price €14, brunch €21, bus largo di torre argentina

(13) Jewish food is the specialty at **Da Giggetto**. Don't miss the deep-fried artichokes, carciofi all giudea, something you can only get (done properly) in this part of town.
via portico d'ottavia 21/a-22, telephone 066 861 105, open tue-sun 12.15pm-3pm, 7.30pm-11pm, price €10, bus largo di torre argentina

(17) The nephews of **Sora Lella** run her restaurant these days. It's elegant but still very welcoming. The brothers stick to what they know - classic Roman cuisine - and a great job they do of it too.
via di ponte quattro capi 16, telephone 066 861 601, open mon-sat 12.45pm-2.30pm, 7.45pm-10.50pm, price €13, bus largo di torre argentina

(30) The **Four XXXX Pub** is not just another pub - it's a music bar, Tex-Mex restaurant and pizzeria all rolled into one. There's a different type of live music every night of the week, from blues to Dixieland to jazz. It's a good place to come either to eat or for drinks and to chill out after dinner. The menu ranges from classic Tex-Mex dishes to burgers and grilled meats, plus pizzas.
via galvani 29, telephone 065 757 296, www.fourxxxxpub.it, open mon-fri noon-3.30pm, 7pm-2am, sat-sun 7pm-2am, price €10, metro piramide

(31) **Ketumbar** is one of the classics of the Via Galvani run. The décor is Indo-Chinese, and the food is influenced from this part of the world as well. This is a good place for a bite to eat or a post-dinner drink to get in the mood before heading off to the clubbing circuit in the neighborhood.
via galvani 24, telephone 065 730 5338, open tue-sun 8pm-midnight, price cocktail €9, metro piramide

(32) Despite its bizarre name, **Tuttifrutti** is actually a no-nonsense trattoria where you can enjoy a selection of ever-changing seasonal dishes for a reasonable price. If you're here on a Friday definitely go for the fish dish of the day.
via luca della robbia 3a, telephone 065 757 902, open tue-sun 8pm-midnight, price €10, metro piramide

Shopping

(3) Bubble, bubble, toil and trouble... The herbs, roots, and mysterious tinctures sold at the **Antica Erboristeria Romana** have a certain element of witchiness about them, even more so because their infusions and remedies seem to work.

via di torre argentina 15, telephone 066 879 493, open mon-sat 9.30am-1.30pm, 2.30pm-7.30pm, bus largo di torre argentina

(4) Design-junky heaven, **Spazio sette** is an entire palace dedicated to the crème-de-la-crème of international interior decorating. From dessert spoons to bookcases, you could fit your pad out completely here, if only you could afford it.

via dei barbieri 7, telephone 066 869 747, open mon 3.30pm-7.30pm, tue-sat 8.30am-1pm, 3.30pm-7.30pm, bus largo di torre argentina

(10) You wouldn't feel you've been on holiday in Italy if you didn't bring back some yummy treats. Why not make them organic? At **Albero del pane** you get olive oil from the Tre Colli farm north of Rome, whose trees have never seen a pesticide or unnatural fertilizer, and you can taste the pure efforts of Mother Nature. There are also organic pasta and sauces, wine, vinegar and prosecco.

via di s. maria del pianto 19, telephone 066 865 016, open mon-sat 9am-7.30pm, bus largo di torre argentina

(11) It's easy to miss this hole-in-the-wall, basement **shoe shop**, which doesn't even have a name, but that would be a shame. It has the latest foot fashion for men and women at bargain prices, from about €15. The constantly changing stock is usually ex-catwalk or sample items.

via portico d'ottavia 57, no telephone, open mon-thu 9am-7.30pm, fri 9.30am-1pm, sun 10am-1pm, 4pm-6pm, bus largo di torre argentina

(12) **Leone Limentani** carries the best quality tableware and kitchen accessories in classic, timeless styles. You might have to ask for assistance because it's easy to get lost in this underground maze.
via portico d'ottavia 47, telephone 066 880 6686 or 066 880 6949, open mon 3.30pm-7.30pm, tue-sat 9am-1pm, 3.30pm-7.30pm, bus largo di torre argentina

㉓ ROSETO COMUNALE

Nice to do

(2) Don't be surprised at the number of cats hanging around this square - they're in the care of the **Torre Argentina Cat Sanctuary**, whose head-quarters are on the southern side of the square. They look after about 400 abandoned and stray cats at any given time.
largo di torre argentina (corner via florida and via di torre argentina), telephone 066 872 133, open mon-sat noon-6pm, sun 2pm-3pm, free guided tours in english sat and sun 3pm, bus largo di torre argentina

(23) The city rose gardens, or **Roseto Comunale**, are a favorite strolling place when the flowers are in bloom from late April to July, especially when the competition gardens are open in June. The gardens are on the site of the former Jewish cemetery, a fact that is commemorated in a menorah-shaped (when seen from above) layout of paths and plants.
entrances in clivo dei pubblici and via di valle murcia, telephone 060 606, open may, june, sept daily 9am-sunset, admission free, metro circo massimo

(24) The Knights of the Order of Malta, originally set up to help Christians on their way to the Holy Land at the time of the crusades, have their own sovereign state in **Piazza Cavalieri di Malta** on the green and peaceful Aventine hill, complete with a head of state, passport-issuing powers and their own license plates. Through the keyhole of the priory door is a singular view of St Peter's in the distance (especially beautiful at night when the dome is lit up).
piazza dei cavalieri di malta 4, telephone 065 779 193, www.orderofmalta.org, metro circo massimo

Largo Argentina, Ghetto & Caracalla

Take a bus to Largo di Torre Argentina ① ②. Browse in some of the near-by shops ③ ④ and restaurants ⑤, then head down to Via delle Botteghe Oscure ⑥ ⑦ ⑧. Turn into Via dei Polacchi, turn right into Via dei Delfini and keep going to Piazza Mattei ⑨. Keep going along Via dei Falegnami, turn left into Via in Publicolis, then turn left again into Via S. Maria del Pianto ⑩. Continue straight to the main street of the ghetto, Via Portico d'Ottavia ⑪ ⑫ ⑬, at the far end of which is Teatro di Marcello ⑭. Follow the street to the right ⑮ and cross the road and the bridge ⑯ ⑰. Backtrack along Via del Portico d'Ottavia and take the tiny street to the right of Da Giggetto, which leads up to Piazza Campitelli. Continue straight along Via Cavaletti, through Piazza Margana and Via Margana, then turn right into Via Ara Coeli which takes you to the stairs to Piazza del Campidoglio ⑱. Up the steps, admire the square and the Musei Capitolini ⑲. Make sure you go to the back end of the square, past Palazzo dei Senatori and under the arch, for a view of the Roman Forum. Turn into Via Monte Tarpeo and Via Tempio di Giove, and follow the paths through the gardens until you come out on Vico Jugario. Turn right and follow Via Petroselli, past the temples on your right and the arch on your left ⑳, until Bocca della Verità ㉑. Turn left after the church and follow Via della Greca to Circo Massimo ㉒. You now have three choices: If you like quiet gardens and picturesque views, cross the road at Piazzale Ugo La Malfa. Follow Via di Valle Murcia past the Roseto comunale ㉓, and keep going along Via di S. Sabina, passing the orange gardens of Parco Savelli until Piazza dei Cavalieri di Malta ㉔. If you haven't had enough of ancient Rome yet, continue straight though Circo Massimo, cross Piazza di Porta Capena ㉕ and keep going down Viale Terme di Caracalla ㉖. If you want to be in a good area for drinks and dinner later on, hop on the metro at Circo Massimo and ride one stop to Piramide. Admire the Pyramid ㉗ and cemetery ㉘, then head towards Monte Testaccio ㉙, where Rome's hippest bars and restaurants stand side by side ㉚ ㉛ ㉜.

1. Area Sacra dell'Argentina
2. Torre Argentina Cat Sanctuary
3. Antica Erboristeria Romana
4. Spazio sette
5. Renato e Luisa
6. Le Bain
7. Crypta Balbi
8. Chiesa del Gesù
9. Piazza Mattei
10. Albero del pane
11. shoe shop
12. Leone Limentani
13. Da Giggetto
14. Teatro di Marcello
15. Sinagoga and Museo della Comunità Ebraica
16. Isola Tiberina
17. Sora Lella
18. Piazza del Campidoglio
19. Musei Capitolini
20. Foro Boario
21. Bocca della Verità
22. Circo Massimo
23. Roseto Comunale
24. Piazza dei Cavalieri di Malta
25. Obelisco di Axum
26. Terme di Caracalla
27. Pyramid
28. Cimitero Acattolico
29. Monte Testaccio
30. Four XXXX Pub
31. Ketumbar
32. Tuttifrutti

⬤ Sights	
⬤ Food & drink	
◯ Shopping	
⬤ Nice to do	

Vatican & Piazza Navona

Rome is a special city for many reasons, but one of its strangest quirks is having an entire separate country in its middle. The Vatican's wealth has been invested in fantastic art works over the centuries, many of which can be seen in the spectacular Musei Vaticani and the Basilica di S. Pietro. If you're not a culture vulture or if you need some distractions, don't despair - the streets around the Vatican, especially Via Ottaviano and Via Cola di Rienzo are full of interesting shops.

Across the river small, winding streets lead to Piazza Navona. Once a stomping ground of young noblemen travelling around Europe on the 'Grand Tour' that was to complete their education, these days it's a favorite area for an afternoon stroll or a night out. On Via del Governo Vecchio you'll

5

find interesting shops, both designer and second hand, and on Piazza Navona there's never a dull moment between people watching, sitting at cafés and admiring the street performers. The square and its surroundings are also packed with beautiful churches, fountains and museums. With all the charming restaurants and bars around, this is a lively part of town in the evening. The only problem is having so much to choose from!

6 Musts!

Basilica di S. Pietro

Be moved by
Michelangelo's Pietà in
the Basilica di S. Pietro.

Castel S. Angelo

Explore the labyrinth of
Castel S. Angelo.

Mandarina Duck

Make it yours:
the latest bag from
Mandarina Duck.

**Antico Caffè
della Pace**

People-watch at the
Antico Caffè della Pace.

Da Baffetto

Get a pizza - and some
abuse - at Da Baffetto.

Piazza Navona

Soak up the atmosphere
of Piazza Navona.

○ **Sights**
○ **Shopping**

● **Food & drink**
● **Nice to do**

Sights

③ While the Sistine Chapel is amazing, it would be a shame not to spare some time for the other parts of the **Musei Vaticani**. There's the picture gallery, ancient Greek and Roman sculptures, extensive Egyptian and Etruscan collections, an ethnological and missionaries' museum, not to mention the decorations of various popes' apartments, such as the Stanze di Raffaello or the Appartamento Borgia. If you plan to take your time here and enjoy the museums to their fullest, allow at least two hours.

viale del vaticano, telephone 066 988 3041, www.vatican.va, open mar-oct mon-fri 8.45am-4.45pm, sat 8.45am-1.45pm, nov-feb mon-sat 8.45am-1.45pm, closed sun except last sun of month free admission 8.45am-1.45pm, admission €10, metro ottaviano - s. pietro

⑨ The **Basilica di S. Pietro**, the epicenter of the Roman Catholic world built on the site of St. Peter's tomb, is the world's biggest church. If you don't believe it - which you might easily not, because it's so perfectly proportioned that you don't actually feel the size - then find the markers down the middle of the floor indicating the size of other major churches in the world. The full height, from the floor to the cross on top of the dome, is 136 meters - nearly three Colosseums stacked on top of each other. The central baldachin, made from bronze stripped from the roof of the Pantheon, is nearly 30 meters tall. While there has been a place of worship here since pre-Christian times, it was Pope Julius II's project, started in 1506, that gave the church its present form. Pope Julius enlisted the help of artists such as Bramante, Raffaelo, Peruzzi, Sangallo and Michelangelo, but didn't live to see his ambitious design for the dome completed. Incredibly moving in all this grandeur is Michelangelo's tender and delicate Pietà, in the first chapel on the right, behind bulletproof glass since it was attacked.

piazza s. pietro, open summer daily 7am-6pm, winter daily 7am-5pm, admission free, decent dress required, metro ottaviano - s. pietro

(10) You shouldn't miss the view from the **Cupola di S. Pietro**, the dome. You can take an elevator to the first viewing platform, then climb up to an inner corridor that takes you around the inside of the dome, and then up more steps to the lantern. Pace yourself - in total, it's over 500 steps.
piazza di s. pietro (entrance just to the right of the portico of the church),
open summer daily 7am-5pm, winter daily 7am-4pm, admission €4, with
use of elevator €5, metro ottaviano - s. pietro

(12) **Castel S. Angelo** was built as the mausoleum for the emperor Hadrian but it has been in almost constant use since the fall of the Roman empire, as a prison, a treasury, a fortress and now a museum. The best way to get a feel for the complex structure is to wander through it from basement to top terrace - from which there is a great view.
lungotevere castello 50, telephone 066 819 111, open tue-sun 9am-8pm,
admission €5, metro ottaviano - s. pietro or lepanto

(14) Pedestrianized **Ponte S. Angelo** is one of the nicest places to cross the Tiber, under the watchful eyes of Bernini's angels bearing signs of Christ's passion. This bridge was built in 1450 to replace the Roman one that had partially collapsed under the weight of pilgrims traveling to Hadrian's tomb during that Jubilee year.
ponte s. angelo, metro ottaviano - s. pietro or lepanto

(22) The church of **S. Maria della Pace** is definitely one of the most picturesque in Rome, with its semicircular portico, and it's always a pleasant surprise when you come around the corner from Piazza Navona and see it squashed into the end of the street. The attached Chiostro del Bramante, where temporary exhibitions are held, seems much bigger than it is.
via della pace, telephone 066 861 156, www.chiostrodelbramante.it, open
irregularly, bus corso rinascimento

㉖ Showplace of artists, favorite destination for an afternoon walk, and generally a great place to hang out, **Piazza Navona** is one of the most popular squares in Rome. The 'square' is actually oval, because it was built on the remains of a Roman circus, the Stadio di Domiziano. You can see some of the remains in the crypt of the church of S. Agnese in Agone, and from the outside of a building on the north end of the square, in Piazza Tor Sanguigna.

piazza navona, bus corso rinascimento

㉗ **FONTANA DEI QUATTRO FIUMI**

㉗ The **Fontana dei Quattro Fiumi** in the middle of Piazza Navona represents the four most important rivers known in the 17th century: the Nile, the Ganges, the Danube, and the Rio Plata, and apart from these majestic river men it's also populated by fantastic beasts, including a horse, a lion, a snake and a really bizarre crocodile. The fountain was designed by Bernini, and there are many legends about the rivalry between the sculptor and the architect Borromini, designer of nearby S. Agnese in Agone. One of the stories says that the river facing the church is holding his hand in fear that the 'ugly' structure will collapse, and that Borromini responded by placing a statue on the most precarious outer ledge nearest the fountain.
piazza navona, bus corso rinascimento

㉘ **S. Agnese in Agone** is allegedly built on the site of the brothel where poor St. Agnes was thrown, naked, for being Christian. Her hair grew miraculously to protect her modesty, and when one of the patrons tried to touch her he was struck down by lightning. It didn't do the girl any good, though, since she was then tortured to death. The church is architecturally very important as an example of Borromini's baroque innovations.
piazza navona, telephone 0668 192 134, open tue-sat 4.30pm-7pm, sun 10am-1pm, bus corso rinascimento

㉚ Part of the Museo Nazionale Roman, the beautiful renaissance **Palazzo Altemps** is a showcase for some of the private collections by noble families of ancient Roman sculpture, most importantly that of the Ludovisi family.
piazza s. apollinare 46, telephone 063 996 7700, open tue-sun 9am-7.45pm, admission €5, bus corso rinascimento

㉛ **Palazzo Braschi** houses the Museo di Roma, where paintings and artifacts illustrate the city's history from the Middle Ages to the 20th century. Here you can get a real feel for what it was like to live in Rome a few hundred years ago, with the help of portraits, scenes of everyday life, and costumes. The splendid palace is worth a visit in its own right, especially the elaborate staircase and the decorated rooms.
via s. pantaleo, telephone 066 710 8346, www.museodiroma.comune.roma.it, open tue-sun 9am-7pm, admission €5, bus corso rinascimento

Food & drink

(2) You don't need a menu to decide what to have at **Il Matriciano** - try the restaurant's namesake, the 'pasta all'amatriciana'. It's amazing that something as simple as a tangy tomato and bacon sauce can taste so good! There's probably a secret ingredient in there somewhere, but they're not telling.
via dei gracchi 55, telephone 063 213 040 or 063 212 327, open summer mon-fri 12.45pm-2.30pm, 8pm-11.30pm, winter mon-tue, thu-sat 12.45pm-2.30pm, 8pm-11.30pm, price €8.50, metro ottaviano - s. pietro

(11) In the close-knit quarter of Borgo Pio, the colorful local characters have always been known by their nicknames. **Il Mozzicone**, which translates to 'the cigarette butt', probably had something different written on his birth certificate, but as a restaurateur he's never been known as anything else. Brace you stomach for heavy and filling Roman meat dishes but take heart - you can take a beautiful digestive walk by St. Peter's afterwards.
borgo pio 180 (corner piazza del catalone), telephone 066 861 500, open mon-sat noon-3pm, 7pm-11pm, price €9, metro ottaviano - s. pietro

(17) **Tonino** is the sort of basic neighborhood trattoria that is getting more rare in cities everywhere these days. This one has been here for three generations and fortunately it doesn't look like it's going anywhere. In an ambience of beaded curtains, paper tablecloths and plastic chairs, you can savor no-nonsense, traditional Italian food as it's meant to be.
via del governo vecchio, telephone 333 587 0779, open mon-sat 1pm-3pm, 8pm-11pm, price €8, bus piazza chiesa nuova

(18) For probably the best pizza in Rome you've got to go to **Da Baffetto**. The waiters are not known for their politeness - they're actually famous for being rude - and it's a bit of a tight squeeze inside. But the long queues outside every day of the week speak for themselves: it's all good-natured fun and the pizza is definitely worth it.
via del governo vecchio 114, telephone 066 861 617, open daily 6.30pm-1am, price €7, bus piazza chiesa nuova

(21) Don your coolest shades and linger over a cappuccino at the **Antico Caffè della Pace** for an entertaining morning of people-watching and soaking up Rome's atmosphere. This café has been here practically since the dawn of time and is still going strong.

via della pace 3-7, telephone 066 861 216, open daily 9am-2am, price cappuccino €3, bus piazza chiesa nuova or corso rinascimento

(23) If you want the 'right' place for an aperitif or a nightcap, head for the **Bar del Fico**, where stars and aspiring stars rub shoulders with local neighborhood eccentrics. It's also a great place to sit under the fig tree and read the newspaper on a Sunday afternoon.

piazza del fico 26/28, telephone 066 865 205, open daily 8am-2am, price drink €4.50, bus piazza chiesa nuova or corso rinascimento

(24) **Il Corallo** is a fine choice for dinner, not just because of the delicious pizza and pasta dishes but also because the young, friendly staff members obviously enjoy their work and make you feel welcome. There are tables outside in the summer on the picturesque little street.

via del corallo 10, telephone 066 830 7703, open tue-sun 7pm-midnight, price €10, bus corso rinascimento

Shopping

(1) **Castroni** is packed to the seams with goodies, both Italian and international. You can savor their delicious, freshly roasted blends of coffee at the bar or browse the shelves for unusual condiments, oils and sweets. The international section is a lifeline for homesick foreigners in Rome.
via ottaviano 55, telephone 0639 723 279, www.castronigroup.it, open mon-sat 8am-8pm, metro ottaviano - s. pietro

(5) At **La Cicogna**, the stork brings babies as well as babies' clothes. With good quality children's clothes by the likes of Armani Junior and Versace Young, the little angels in your life will look as cute as buttons.
via cola di rienzo 268, telephone 066 821 0683, open mon 3.30pm-7.30pm, tue-sat 10am-7.30pm, metro ottaviano - s. pietro

(6) The brainchild of a couple of Italian designers, **Mandarina Duck** specializes in accessories, mainly bags, in brightly colored leather and plastic. The unusual, last-a-lifetime pieces don't come cheap, but think of them as worthwhile investments.
via cola di rienzo 270-272, telephone 066 896 491, www.mandarinaduck.com, open mon 3.30pm-7.30pm, tue-sat 10am-1.30pm, 3.30pm-7.30pm, metro ottaviano - s. pietro

(7) Silk, cotton and cashmere are the order of the day at **Blunauta**, which has gone somewhat upmarket in recent years since its warehouse, stock-price origins. It's a good place to look for bargains and unusual styles.
via cola di rienzo 303-308, telephone 063 9737 336, open 10am-8pm, sun 10am-2pm, 4pm-8pm, metro ottaviano - s. pietro

(8) **Halfon** isn't the most exciting shop in the world, but it's good for sharp dressers who want to pick up a few stylish pieces for their work wardrobe. Be warned, though - in Italy, women's business suits can have much, much shorter skirts than you'd find in many other countries.
via cola di rienzo, telephone 066 834 059, open mon 3.30pm-7.30pm, tue-sat 10am-1pm, 3.30pm-7.30pm, metro ottaviano - s. pietro

(15) The unadulterated colors, textures and styles of India await you at **FabIndia**. If you want something somewhat unusual and incredibly comfortable you'll find it here, along with helpful instructions on how to wear these outlandish garments. We'll never know if it they're hot off the Delhi catwalk or last season's rejects, but if they appeal, who cares?
via del banco di s. spirito 40, telephone 066 889 1230, open mon 3pm-7.30pm, tue-sat 10am-1.30pm and 3pm-7.30pm, bus piazza chiesa nuova

(16) There's no such thing as having too many shoes, so why not stop off at **Impronta** to check out the latest designs? The beautifully made footwear is sure to add a touch of glamor to every girl's outfit.
via del governo vecchio 1-2, telephone 066 896 947, open mon 3.30pm-7.30pm, tue-sat 9.30am-7.30pm, bus piazza chiesa nuova

(19) **Brandy** carries great casual and sporty clothes for the hip and young at heart. Rummage through the racks of prettily colored trousers, shirts and jumpers and you're sure to find some real bargains.
via sora 33, telephone 066 871 268, open mon 3.30pm-7.30pm, tue-sat 10am-1.30pm, 3.30pm-7.30pm, bus piazza chiesa nuova

(20) For a dramatic outfit that just may have people asking for your autograph, you've got to stop by **Maga Morgana**. Luciana Iannace started out as a costume designer, and her outfits are still favored by Italian starlets. From evening dresses to cool daywear, shoes and hats, everything here will put you on center stage.
via del governo vecchio 27 and 98, telephone 066 879 995 or 066 878 095, open mon-sat 10am-8pm, bus piazza chiesa nuova

(25) Chances are you won't be able to walk past **Too Much** without pausing for a peek. What do they sell? Wild and wacky home accessories, weird but amusing stationery, mildly amusing sex toys - things for people who have everything. A favorite with passing pilgrims are the wind-up nun figurines.
via s. maria dell'anima 29, telephone 066 830 1187, open daily noon-1am, bus corso rinascimento

MAGA MORGANA ⓪

Nice to do

(4) You can actually visit the seemingly remote **Giardini Vaticani** quite easily, albeit only in guided group tours, by booking with the pilgrim information office. The carefully landscaped gardens, which center on the Casina Pius IV, a garden chateau, are a haven of peace and a peek behind Vatican walls.
ufficio informazioni pellegrini e turisti (piazza s. pietro, on the left side), telephone 066 988 4466 or 066 988 4866, visits (mar-mid-oct) mon-tues, thurs, fri, sat 10am-noon, (nov-feb) sat only, admission €9, metro ottaviano - s. pietro

(13) The park around the mausoleum of Hadrian, the **Parco Adriano**, is on two levels. On the lower level children run and people take their dogs to play, while the upper level has benches under shady trees, and in the summer there are book fairs and concerts here.
castel s. angelo, open sunrise-sunset, admission free, metro ottaviano - s. pietro, bus piazza chiesa nuova

(29) Piazza Navona is one of the places where you can take a **horse-drawn carriage ride** for a unique tour of Rome. The tours takes in the major monuments of Rome and cost in the region of €100 - and you can talk to the fiercely proud drivers about what you'd like to see.
piazza navona, bus corso rinascimento

(32) Piazza Navona is a stage for numerous **street performers**, ranging from acrobats to inexplicably popular statue people, clowns, mimes and musicians. A perennial favorite is Marcel, whose miniature finger puppets impersonate Charlie Chaplin and Michael Jackson.
piazza navona, bus corso rinascimento

Vatican & Piazza Navona

Coming out of the metro station Ottaviano - S. Pietro, take the far left-hand exit marked Via Ottaviano. Head down that shop-lined street - getting a coffee at Castroni ①, corner Via Germanico, if you want - past Via dei Gracchi ② to Piazza Risorgimento. Either follow the Vatican walls on the right to the entrance of the Musei Vaticani ③ ④, or turn left into Via Cola di Rienzo for some light shopping first ⑤ ⑥ ⑦ ⑧. The Musei Vaticani lead out to the foot of the Basilica di S. Pietro ⑨, where you should definitely join the line to go up into the Cupola ⑩. Exit into the square and go through the colonnade on the left, exit through the gate into Via Porta Angelica and turn right into Borgo Pio. Get some lunch at Il Mozzicone ⑪ or turn right after the restaurant into Via Tre Pupazze and get back onto Via della Conciliazione, which leads you to Castel S. Angelo ⑫ ⑬. Then cross Ponte S. Angelo ⑭ into Banco di S. Spirito ⑮, and turn right into Via Banchi Nuovi, which becomes Via del Governo Vecchio ⑯ ⑰. At the corner of Via Sora is Da Baffetto ⑱, and up that street is Brandy ⑲. Continue another block along Via del Governo Vecchio ⑳ and then turn left into Via Teatro Pace; to the left you'll hit a nightlife strip that includes the Antico Caffe della Pace ㉑ and Piazza del Fico ㉓, off which leads Via del Corallo ㉔. At the end of Via della Pace is the church of S. Maria della Pace ㉒. If instead you turn right into Via di Tor Millina ㉕ you'll come out in Piazza Navona ㉖, where you'll want to have a closer look at the Fontana dei Quattro Fiumi ㉗ and S. Agnese in Agone ㉘. Now it's up to you - do you want some more museums? Head to the top end of the piazza, past the horses ㉙ and out through Via Agonale, crossing the road into Piazza S. Apollinare where Palazzo Altemps ㉚ is. Or head to the south end of the square, through Piazza Pasquino to the entrance of Palazzo Braschi ㉛. If you've had enough for the day, just chill out and watch the street performers ㉜.

1. Castroni
2. Il Matriciano
3. Musei Vaticani
4. Giardini Vaticani
5. La Cicogna
6. Mandarina Duck
7. Blunauta
8. Halfon
9. Basilica di S. Pietro
10. Cupola di S. Pietro
11. Il Mozzicone
12. Castel S. Angelo
13. Parco Adriano
14. Ponte S. Angelo
15. Fabindia
16. Impronta
17. Tonino
18. Da Baffetto
19. Brandy
20. Maga Morgana
21. Antico Caffè della Pace
22. S. Maria della Pace
23. Bar del Fico
24. Il Corallo
25. Too Much
26. Piazza Navona
27. Fontana dei Quattro Fiumi
28. S. Agnese in Agone
29. Horse-drawn carriage ride
30. Palazzo Altemps
31. Palazzo Braschi
32. Street performers

○ Sights
● Food & drink
○ Shopping
● Nice to do

Campo de' Fiori & Trastevere

There's something going on around Piazza Campo de' Fiori at all times of the day and night. Whether it's market stalls in the morning, shoppers in the afternoon, or diners and night owls later on, there's a permanently energetic atmosphere. Take your pick of traditional or trendy restaurants and bars - there's something for all tastes. Also, don't miss out on the shopping in Via dei Baullari and Via dei Giubbonari, where there's a good mix of casual and chic boutiques.

Trastevere, on the other side of the Tiber, feels like an independent village. But don't let the sleepy daytime atmosphere mislead you into thinking you're in the provinces: at night you can hardly move on the narrow streets, they're so packed with revelers. Between historic churches and restaurants that

6

have been here as long as anyone can remember, there's plenty of room for a lively, often-changing bar scene. Two other features are important on this side of the river. The Porta Portese flea market is a great place to spend a Sunday morning, provided that you watch your wallet in the crowds. The Janiculum (Gianicolo) hill towers over Trastevere, and from the piazza at its summit you can enjoy a great view.

6 Musts!

Piazza Campo de' Fiori

Buy some fresh fruit at the market of Piazza Campo de' Fiori.

L'Angolo Divino

Have a glass of wine at L'Angolo Divino.

S. Cecilia

Get spooked by the fate of poor, steamed alive S. Cecilia.

S. Maria in Trastevere

Marvel at the mosaics of S. Maria in Trastevere.

Porta Portese

Rummage through the stalls of Porta Portese fleamarket.

Il Gianicolo

Feel on top of the world on the Gianicolo hill.

○ Sights
○ Shopping

● Food & drink
● Nice to do

Sights

(1) **Chiesa Nuova**, the new church, was home to the order of S. Filippo Neri, the holy man who was one of the Counter-Reformation's most popular representatives. The pope recognized the 'Oratorians', as they were known, in 1574 and gave them the dilapidated church of S. Maria in Vallicella as their home. The brothers had the church rebuilt following the model of the brand new Chiesa del Gesù nearby (see Chapter 4, (8)). During the following century elaborate decorations were added, including lively ceiling frescoes by Pietro da Cortona and beautiful paintings by Peter Paul Rubens over the main altar.

piazza della chiesa nuova, telephone 066 875 289, open daily 10.30am-noon, 5pm-6pm, bus piazza chiesa nuova

(5) **Palazzo della Cancelleria** was built as a home for Cardinal Raffaele Riario in the early 1500s, but it was confiscated soon after to house the Papal Chancellery. You can't visit the building, but do take a moment to nip into the beautiful courtyard, which was designed by Bramante. By doing so you're stepping into another country, because the building is an extraterritorial part of the Vatican. Cardinal Riario didn't think anything of knocking down the 4th-century Basilica of S. Lorenzo in Damaso, one of the most important early Christian churches of Rome, to make room for his home, but the pope was furious and made him rebuild it nearby.

piazza della cancelleria, church entrance in corso vittorio emanuele II, no telephone, not open to public, bus piazza chiesa nuova

(10) The French did well to secure **Palazzo Farnese** as the seat of their embassy - they could hardly have found a more beautiful building or square. The palace was commissioned in 1517, but it took over 60 years and a string of illustrious architects including Michelangelo and Giacomo della Porta, to complete it. The granite tubs that decorate the square as fountains once stood in the Baths of Caracalla (Chapter 4, (26)).

piazza farnese, no telephone, not open for visits, bus piazza chiesa nuova

(17) **Galleria Spada** in the lovely Palazzo Spada contains mainly Italian works from the 16th and 17th centuries, and has kept the characteristics of a private collection, being set up more for decorative value than by any artistic logic. The palazzo is famous for its optical illusion, a 9-meter colonnade that looks about four times that length, designed by Borromini with the help of a mathematician.

piazza capo di ferro 13, telephone 066 861 158, www.galleriaborghese.it, open tue-sat 9am-7pm, sun and holidays 8.30am-1pm, admission €5, bus piazza chiesa nuova

(21) The people of Trastevere consider themselves to be the most Roman of the Romans, and you can see some of the foundations of that local culture at the **Museo di Roma in Trastevere**. The permanent collection includes paintings of the city and manuscripts of Rome's most popular vernacular poets.

piazza s. egidio 1/b, telephone 065 816 563, www.comune.roma.it/museo-diroma.trastevere, open tue-sun 10am-8pm, admission €2.90 plus exhibition charge, tram viale trastevere

(22) The convent of the church of **S. Maria della Scala** houses a **pharmaceutical museum** with equipment from the 17th century. Downstairs, the modern-day pharmacy has kept much of its original design, with frescoed ceilings and wooden cabinets. You can still buy some of the old apothecary's concoctions - anyone in need of some 'hysteria water'?

piazza di s. maria della scala, telephone 065 806 233, church open mon-sat 7am-8am, 4.30pm-6.30pm, sun 7.15am-8.15am, 10.30am-12.30pm, 4.30pm-6.30pm, admission free, visits to pharmaceutical museum call for appointment tel. 329 622 3401, admission free, tram viale trastevere

(24) If the baroque art of Rome is starting to grate on your nerves, you might want to take refuge in Palazzo Corsini, which houses the **Galleria Nazionale d'Arte Antica**. The national collection of 16th and 17th century paintings has important works by Italians and foreigners, including Rubens and Van Dyck, and on the canvasses you can see the early tendencies of an anti-baroque classicism.

via della lungara 10, telephone 066 880 2323, www.galleriaborghese.it, open tue-fri 9am-7pm, sat 9am-2pm, sun and national holidays 9am-1pm, admission €4, tram viale trastevere

㉕ **Villa Farnesina** is a joy to visit for many reasons: the harmonious Renaissance architecture, the formal gardens, the vivid optical illusions of Peruzzi and the delicate frescoes by Raffaelo. Who knows what the man who commissioned the villa was like, the wealthy banker Agostino Chigi - what sort of a man has frescoes of his wife preparing herself for their wedding in one room, while paintings of his naked mistress frolicking with Cupid and Psyche adorn the ceiling of another? But you can't argue with the guy's taste in artists - the mythological scenes by Raffaelo in the Sala di Galatea are exceptional, and the Salone delle Prospettive tricks your eye into seeing a panorama of 16th-century Rome.

via della lungara 230, telephone 066 998 0313, http://web.lincei.it/villafarnesina, open mon-sat 9am-1pm, admission €4.50, tram viale trastevere

26 The undisputed heart of Trastevere is the church of **S. Maria in Trastevere**. It is believed to have been the first official Christian place of worship constructed after the legalization of this religion in the 4th century. The site was not chosen haphazardly: in 38 BC, on the spot where the main altar of the church is now, a stream of oil, the fons olei gushed from the ground for one day, and this was retrospectively interpreted as a sign of the coming of Christ. The present structure dates mostly from the 12th century, including the awe-inspiring, gold-glittering mosaic of the Virgin and Child with ten attendant women on the façade. The church was built with the help of materials looted from the baths of Caracalla (see Chapter 4, number 26), and the 12 columns inside are all ancient. The mosaics in the apse behind the main altar show scenes from the life of Mary.

piazza di s. maria in trastevere, open daily 7am-noon and 3pm-7pm, admission free, tram viale trastevere

30 According to legend, the **Basilica di S. Cecilia** was built on the site of S. Cecilia's house, where the saint was martyred to death in the 3rd century. The story goes that Cecilia, a devout Christian and active converter, was condemned to being steamed to death in the hot baths of her own house. Three days in the hot rooms didn't hurt her, so the Roman prefect had her beheaded instead, but despite his best efforts the executioner couldn't fully separate her head from her body, and she lived another three days. Apparently she sang throughout her ordeal, leading her to become the patron saint of music. The church was built in the 9th century, but adjustments to the façade are from the 1200s, and the inside is mostly 17th century. You can visit the Roman remains underneath the church too.

piazza di s. cecilia 22, telephone 065 899 289, open daily 9.30am-12.30pm and 4pm-6.30pm, admission free, tram viale trastevere

Food & drink

(2) Romans wax lyrical about the **Pasticceria Napoletana**, a Neapolitan bakery and pastry shop specializing in southern Italian sweets. Judge for yourself if this amount of excitement over pastries is justified - chances are, you'll agree. This is a good place for a sugar-rich breakfast.
corso vittorio emanuele II, telephone 066 877 048, open 7am-8.30pm, coffee €0.70, bus piazza chiesa nuova

(4) The cute and cozy interior of **Al Bric** invites passersby to stop in for something to eat and a glass of wine. With tasteful attention to detail - fresh flowers, panels from wine crates on the walls, an open kitchen - you can feel really comfortable here. The food is hearty, and there is also an excellent cheese board.
via del pellegrino 51-52, telephone 066 879 533, open tue-sun 7.30pm-11.30pm, price €14, bus piazza chiesa nuova

(6) If you want to chill out over some mellow music and a well-mixed cocktail, the guys and gals at **Criscanimagiu** won't let you down. Added bonuses are good salads and couscous dishes, and live jazz music on Thursday nights in the summer.
piazza della cancelleria 87, telephone 066 830 8888, open daily 7am-2am, price snack €6, bus largo di torre argentina

(7) Rome's first feng shui restaurant, **Agua**, is designed to allow energy to circulate freely according to ancient Chinese wisdom. Make up your own mind whether that's just a gimmick or there's actually some truth in it, but the fact is that the three floors of minimalist, white and cream colored furnishings are very striking and provide a pleasant atmosphere to spend an evening. Food is Italian-Mediterranean with a hint of oriental spices.
piazza della cancelleria 64, telephone 066 830 1162, open wine bar section tue-sun 7pm-2am, restaurant daily 12.30pm-3pm, 7.30pm-11pm, price €13, bus largo di torre argentina

(11) A glass of wine and a little something to nibble on at **L'Angolo Divino** never go amiss, especially the wines by the glass matched with unusual cheeses and cold meats. The wine bar is decorated with dark wooden shelves and lit with romantic candles.
via dei balestrari 12, telephone 066 864 413, open daily 10am-2.30pm, 5pm-1am, price €8, bus largo di torre argentina

(18) Part café, part restaurant, part cocktail bar, **Friends** has something for every time of day and every mood. Whether you want to relax at the end of the day over a drink and some snacks, start the day with an ample breakfast, or enjoy the music and a cocktail in the wee hours, in this high tech ambience of plexiglass and brushed steel you really can't go wrong.
piazza trilussa 34, telephone 065816111, open mon-sat 7am-2am, sun 6pm-2am, price €6, tram viale trastevere

(19) If you prefer stylish and elegant to simple and familiar surroundings, then **Ferrara** is perfect for a special evening out. The wine 'lists', actually inch-thick files of labels, are not for the indecisive. The food might seem bland to some, but it has a difficult task in fitting harmoniously with the many wines on offer.
via del moro 1a / piazza trilussa 41, telephone 065 833 3920, open summer mon-sat 10am-midnight, winter tue-sun 10am-midnight, price €14, tram viale trastevere

(20) **Checco er Carrettiere** is the place to go for Roman cuisine in a traditional setting. The restaurant has been going strong for decades (in the 1950s and 60s it was especially popular with actors and celebrities) and it's still a well-established favorite today.
via benedetta 10-13, telephone 065 817 018, open mon-sat 12.30pm-3pm, 7.30pm-11.15pm, sun 12.30pm-3pm, price €12, tram viale trastevere

(27) From film directors to civil servants, students to market vendors, everyone comes through the **Bar S. Calisto** at some time. It's one of the few, quite possibly the only, places in Trastevere that hasn't changed since that part of town became fashionable, and it's got the cheapest beer in the area. What more can you ask?
piazza s. calisto 3-5, telephone 065 835 869, open mon-sat 6am-1.30am, tram viale trastevere

(31) The atmosphere at the **Taverna dei Mercanti** is quite unusual, with flickering torches outside and echoing, vaulted ceilings inside. A bit Gothic, perhaps, if it weren't for the jolly atmosphere and popularity of the place. You can't go wrong if you stick to traditional Roman dishes or if you're a meat-lover. If you want to spend a little less, go with the pizza menu.
piazza dei mercanti 3a, telephone 065 881 693, open tue-sun 8pm-midnight, price €12, tram viale trastevere

③ ECOLE DE

Shopping

③ A repository of silly gadgets, **Ecole de** is fun for browsing and wondering whatever designers will come up with next. Apart from household accessories, there are also some wearable things (calling moose-shaped backpacks and Astroturf flip-flops 'clothes' is going too far) and, for want of a better word, general fun and unusual gift items.

vicolo della moretta 10-11, telephone 066 892 015, open mon 3pm-8pm, tue-sun 10am-8pm, bus piazza chiesa nuova

⑨ The shoes, boots and sandals at **Shape** are always a bit different than what you see in other shops. The carefully selected, Italian-made models are worth spending a bit more on to have you stepping out in style.

via dei baullari 18, telephone 066 880 6879, open mon 3.30pm-7.30pm, tue-sat 10am-1.30pm, 3.30pm-7.30pm, bus largo di torre argentina

⑫ The colorful, smart clothes at **Ethic** make good outfits for work without being boring. You can mix and match skirts, trousers and tops with coats and jackets. The knitwear is good quality and there is also a small selection of eveningwear.

piazza cairoli 11, telephone 066 830 1063, open mon-sat 10am-1.30pm, 4pm-8pm, bus largo di torre argentina

⑬ There are two distinct sides to **Momento**, the formal and the informal. The evening dresses are colorful and fun, with possibilities of mixing and matching between bodices and skirts if you want a wilder look. The trademark of the shop's own line in casual wear is heavy fabrics, especially corduroy, tweed and brocade, mixed together with lighter materials in unusual skirts, trousers and coats.

piazza b. cairoli 9, telephone 066 880 8157, open mon-fri 9.30am-7.30pm, sat 9.30am-1pm and 3.30pm-7.30pm, bus largo di torre argentina

(14) **Ibiz** is a shop run by a couple of self-taught leather artisans who really know how to work magic with a bit of animal skin. The handbags, briefcases, wallets and belts don't come cheap, but the classic designs and excellent quality will last a lifetime.

via dei chiavari 39, telephone 066 830 7297, open mon-sat 9.30am-7.30pm, bus largo di torre argentina

(15) **Lei** has high quality, feminine clothes guaranteed to make you feel like a million euros. The windows usually concentrate on colorful and unusual evening dresses, but you can find classic suits and casual wear inside as well. Polish off your look with a perfectly matched accessory.

via dei giubbonari 103, telephone 066 875 432, open mon-sat 10am-1.30pm, 3.30pm-7.30pm, bus largo di torre argentina

(16) If you're one for color coordinating outfits down to the footwear, then have a look at the rainbow windows of **Borrini**. The shop owner bases his handmade models on the season's trends, but offers them in a greater variety of colors than other stores and often in better quality too.
via dei pettinari 86-87, telephone 066 875 670, open mon 3.30pm-7pm, tue-sat 9am-1pm, 4pm-8pm, bus largo di torre argentina

(28) **Bibli** is an all around useful address for travelers, offering books, food and internet points. The books are mostly in Italian, but there are a few shelves dedicated to English, French and German writing. The international weekend brunch in the pretty covered courtyard is enough to keep you going all day.
via dei fienaroli 28, telephone shop 065 884 097, cafe 065 814 534, www.bibli.it, open mon 5.30pm-midnight, tue-sun 11am-midnight, price brunch €15.50, tram viale trastevere

(29) If you like cookies, then don't miss **Biscottificio Innocenti**. It's not a fancy shop, in fact, it's really just the front end of a very old bakery, where every available surface is piled high with platters of aromatic goodies. What makes these cookies so special? Maybe it's the ingredients, maybe the family recipes, maybe just the good dose of eccentricity that makes the shop owners so lovable and irreplaceable.
via della luce 21, telephone 065 803 926, open mon-sat 5am-8pm, tram viale trastevere

(33) Soap that's good enough to eat is what you get at **Soapvillage**, a small, colorful shop that is quite new in the neighborhood. It's sold in slices or blocks containing pretty patterns, fresh-looking fruit, abstract designs or funky glitter. They have suds for every occasion, be it birthdays, weddings, Halloween or Christmas.
via a. bertani 1, telephone 065 818 445, www.segniesogni.it, open mon 4pm-8pm, tue-sat 10am-1p, 4pm-8.30pm, tram viale trastevere

Nice to do

(8) The market of **Campo de' Fiori** isn't the cheapest in town, but residents of the historic center generally don't mind paying a bit extra for the upkeep of their local market. How can you not be charmed by the sea of colorful fruit and vegetables, the headstrong, noisy vendors and all the vitality and character of an Italian marketplace? If you can walk through without taking a photo or buying a snack, it's your loss!
piazza campo de' fiori, mon-sat 8am-2pm, bus piazza chiesa nuova

(23) Not in the same league as botanical gardens in other European capitals, but lovely in its own right, the **Orto Botanico** is known mainly to the residents of the area. A beautiful place to spend a morning...
largo cristina da svezia, telephone 068 300 937, open tue-sat 9am-5.30pm, admission €2.07, tram viale trastevere

(32) Bargain hunters will love **Porta Portese fleamarket**, where you might have your wallet stolen but at least you'll be able to buy it back at another stall further down the street. The market has been famous for decades, and although there's quite a bit of imported stuff these days it still maintains its colorful character.
from piazza di porta portese down via portuense, open sun morning, tram viale trastevere

(34) If your feet are up to it, take an hour or so to go for a walk on the **Gianicolo**, the Janiculum hill. The winding paths take you past the Fontana dell'Acqua Paola, a popular spot for wedding photos. On the summit of the hill is Piazza G. Garibaldi, a lookout point with puppet theater and snack stalls. At sunset, this is a very romantic spot but if you're there at midday beware: at noon every day a cannon is fired from just under the piazza, it'll make you jump if you're not expecting it.
bus piazza g. garibaldi

Campo de' Fiori & Trastevere

Get a bus to Piazza Chiesa Nuova (1), cross the street to Pasticceria Napoletana (2) and into tiny Via dei Cartari. Ahead is Via della Moretta (3) and turn right into Via del Pellegrino (4) (5) (6) (7) into Piazza Campo de' Fiori (8). Stroll around the market and the side streets, such as Via dei Baullari, for some shopping (9). Piazza Farnese (10) is next to Campo de' Fiori. With your back to Palazzo Farnese take the top right-hand street leading from the square to l'Angolo Divino (11) to (12) (13) (14) (15). Turn into Via Arco del Monte, towards the river, detouring down Via Capo di Ferro (just before Borrini (16)) to Galleria Spada (17). Via Arco del Monte becomes Via dei Pettinari to Ponte Sisto. On the other side of the river are Friends (18) and Ferrara (19), behind which, in Via Benedetta, is the famous Checco er Carrettiere (20). From Piazza Trilussa the classic evening stroll takes you down Vicolo del Cinque, to Museo di Roma in Trastevere (21). If you want some nature and culture, turn right into Via della Scala (22), keep going straight through the city gate along Via della Lungara. Turn left for the Botanical Gardens (23) or keep going for Galleria Corsini (24) and Villa Farnesina (25). Backtrack to Piazza S. Egidio and turn left for Bar S. Calisto (26). Just off the main square is Piazza S. Calisto (27), from which Via Arco di S. Calisto branches off to Via dei Fienaroli (28). Cutting through Piazza S. Rufino to get onto Via della Lungaretta, turn right and keep going straight across Viale Trastevere. Nip down Via della Luce for some unbeatable cookies (29); then take Via dei Genovesi until it meets Via di S. Cecilia (30). The church is right around the corner from picturesque Piazza dei Mercanti (31). If fleamarkets are your thing, then go straight down Via S. Michele to Piazza di Porta Portese (32). Otherwise take Via S. Madonna dell'Orto and Via Anicia to Piazza S. Francesco D'Assisi and follow Via di S. Francesco a Ripa back across Viale Trastevere. Via Natale del Grande takes you to the colorful market at Piazza S. Cosimato; Via Santini, where Soap Village (33) is nearby. Provided your legs will still carry you, you can now take a walk up the Gianicolo Hill (34) for some of the best views of Rome.

1. Chiesa Nuova
2. Pasticceria Napoletana
3. Ecole de
4. Al Bric
5. Palazzo della Cancelleria
6. Criscanimagiu
7. Aqua
8. Campo de' Fiori
9. Shape
10. Palazzo Farnese
11. L'Angolo Divino
12. Ethic
13. Momento
14. Ibiz
15. Lei
16. Borrini
17. Galleria Spada
18. Friends
19. Ferrara
20. Checco er Carrettiere
21. Museo di Roma in Trastevere
22. S. Maria della Scala +
   pharmaceutical museum
23. Orto Botanico
24. Galleria Nazionale d'Arte Antica
25. Villa Farnesina
26. S. Maria in Trastevere
27. Bar S. Calisto
28. Bibli
29. Biscottificio Innocenti
30. Basilica di S. Cecilia
31. Taverna dei Mercanti
32. Porta Portese fleamarket
33. Soapvillage
34. Gianicolo hill

Legend

- ● Sights
- ● Food & drink
- ○ Shopping
- ● Nice to do

Sights outside the city center

No guidebook can fully cover the Eternal City, and although we've tried to give you a good start there are plenty more things to see. You can find the letters on the overview map in the front of the book

(L) **S. Giovanni in Laterano** is the cathedral of Rome and the pope's seat as the bishop of the city. It was founded by emperor Constantine in the 4th century, and has been remodelled many times since. It's a vast and beautiful church and only the pope can say mass from its central altar, above which a reliquary supposedly contains the heads of Sts. Peter and Paul. There is a lovely cloister, and the octagonal, domed Baptistry has splendid mosaics.
piazza di s. giovanni in laterano, telephone 066 988 6452, church open daily 7am-7pm, cloister open mon-fri 7am-6pm, sat-sun 7am-7pm, museum mon-fri 9am-5pm, admission to cloister and museum €2, metro s. giovanni.
On the northeastern side of the piazza is an important building for pilgrims, housing the **Scala Santa** or holy staircase. It is believed that these 28 steps originally stood in the palace of Pontius Pilate and that Christ walked on them. Pilgrims ascend the stairs on their knees in the hope of gaining plenary indulgence.
s. piazza di s. giovanni in laterano, telephone 067 049 4619, open summer 6.15am-noon, 3.30pm-6.45pm, winter 6.15am-noon, 3pm-6.15pm, metro s. giovanni

(M) The **Terme di Diocelziano**, the baths of Diocletian, were built at the end of the 3rd century and were the largest baths of their day. Diocletian was known for his persecution of Christians and many slaves of this faith died in the construction work. In the 16th century an ageing Michelangelo was commissioned by the pope to design a church, **S. Maria degli Angeli**, within the bath complex. The 91-meter-long strip along the floor of the church marks Rome's meridian and a strategically placed hole in the ceiling allows the sun's rays to tell the time fairly accurately.
piazza della repubblica, telephone 063 996 7700, open tue-sun 9am-7.45pm, admission €5, metro repubblica

VIA APPIA ANTICA Ⓟ

(N) Rome's Pompeii is **Ostia Antica**, the archaeological remains of an ancient port town. You can really get a feel for what life must have been like for the 50,000 people who lived here from the 4th century BC onwards. Visitors are treated to the remains of houses, shops, baths, temples and a splendid amphitheatre. It's just a 20-minute train ride from central Rome and you can round off the day with a seafood lunch in nearby Lido di Ostia, Rome's beach resort.

ostia antica, entrance in via dei romagnoli 717, telephone 065 635 8099, www.ostia-antica.org, open summer tue-sun 9am-6pm, winter tue-sun 9am-4pm, admission €4, train ostia antica (from metro piramide)

(O) Although there are many ancient treasures in Rome, architecture buffs shouldn't miss the relatively modern structures of **EUR**. The initials stand for Esposizione Universale Roma, as Mussolini intended the area to be the site for the universal exhibition of 1942. The enormous, angular, white buildings are impressive; especially eye-catching is the 'square Colosseum', the Palazzo della Civiltà del Lavoro. There are also a number of important museums in EUR, including the Museo Nazionale delle Arti e Tradizioni Popolari, dedicated to Italian folk art and customs, the Museo Nazionale Preistorico-Etnologico Luigi Pigorini, with interesting collections dedicated to the cultures of different continents, and the Museo Nazionale dell'Alto Medioevo, which has tools and utensils from the 4th to the 10th centuries. The Museo della Civiltà Romana brings together plaster casts of Roman treasures scattered around the world.

- *eur, metro eur palasport or eur fermi*
- *museo nazionale delle arti e tradizioni popolari, piazza marconi 10, telephone 065926148 or 065 912 669, www.eur2000.it, open tue-fri 9am-7pm, sat-sun 9am-8pm*
- *museo nazionale preistorico-etnologico luigi pigorini, viale lincoln 14, telephone 063 996 7700, www.pigorini.arti.beniculturali.it, open mon-sun 9am-8pm*
- *museo nazionale dell'alto medioevo, viale lincoln 3, telephone 065 422 8199, open tue-sun 9am-7.30pm*
- *museo della civiltà romana, piazza g. agnelli 10, telephone 065 926 135, open tue-sat 8.30am-6.45pm, sun and holidays 9am-1.30pm*

(P) **Via Appia Antica** was one of the most important consular roads of ancient Rome. You can visit the early Christian catacombs (not for the claustrophobic), admire funeral monuments of Roman nobles and visit a few ancient palaces. This is a wonderful place to go cycling on a sunny day - bikes can be rented at the information center at the beginning of the road (see website). A special shuttle bus, the 'Archeobus', departs hourly between 9am and 5pm from the central Piazza Venezia, and you can buy a hop-on-hop-off ticket to see the ancient road and the natural park that surrounds it. *via appia antica (starts at porta s. sebastiano), telephone for bus info 064 695 4695, telephone for park info 065 126 314, www.parcoappiaantica.org*

Nightlife

Information on what's happening in Rome can be found in *Roma C'è* (a weekly publication) and in the monthly *Time Out*. For information on classical music, look at the fortnightly English publication *Wanted in Rome*. All these are available from newsagents. A good website with tips on clubs and bars is *www.2night.it*. The city council's cultural web pages - *www.comune.roma.it/ cultura* - also have useful information, especially in the summer when open-air festivals abound.

Clubs in Rome get going from about midnight, but most open at about 11pm if you want to skip the line. Bouncers choose the best-dressed people for admission - sneakers are definitely not allowed. Admission prices can be quite steep, from about €15 to €20, but these often include the first drink. Some organizations, especially live music clubs, require that you become a member - this means a one-off charge in addition to the ticket for the event. You can find the letters on the overview map in the front of the book.

Live music

(Q) Rome's new auditorium, the **Auditorium Parco della Musica**, hosts live concerts of every genre. This is also the home of the Accademia di S. Cecilia, Rome's most important classical music organization. If you are a fan of modern architecture this music complex, designed by Renzo Piano, is a pleasure to see and experience and is worth a visit in its own right. Three enormous, scarab beetle-like halls cluster around a central amphitheater, while in the foyer there is a stylish restaurant and wine bar. Guided tours are available daily and the site of an ancient Roman villa discovered during construction can also be visited.

via pietro de coubertin 30, www.musicaperroma.it, tram 2 from piazza del popolo, bus m from termini

(R) **Alexanderplatz** is one of Rome's (and Italy's) best-established clubs for live jazz music. Daily concerts include the biggest Italian and international names. The small, cellar-like ambience is very intimate, but since this is not a large venue it is important to make reservations for important concerts. In the summer, Alexanderplatz helps organize a jazz festival in the beautiful park of Villa Celimontana near the Colosseum.

via ostia 9 (prati), telephone 063 974 2171, www.romajazz.com, doors open 9pm (concert times vary), metro ottaviano

(S) For live blues and rock music the place to go is **Big mama** in lively Trastevere. There are concerts here almost every night, ranging from established and emerging artists, both Italian and foreign. Reservations are recommended - there are only about 50 seats.

vicolo s. francesco a ripa 18, 065 812 551, www.bigmama.it, doors open 9pm, concerts start 10.30pm, tram viale trastevere

Discos & clubs

(T) Calling all hep cats and cool chicks! Just off the Via Veneto, **Jackie O'** beckons with its plush piano bar and disco… this is pure nostalgic elegance, reminiscent of the Rat Pack era. A drink here will set you back a bit, but you'll be rubbing shoulders with international jet setters, minor aristocracy and well-heeled, Armani-clad Italians.
via boncompagni 11, telephone 064 288 5457, open tue-sun 8.30pm-4am, metro barberini

(U) **Goa** is known for creating trends rather than following them. Founding DJ Giancarlino, who takes to the decks every Thursday night, has his finger on the pulse of avant-garde house and electronic music. Friday and Saturday nights are somewhat less experimental, featuring popular international DJs often before they become mainstream in Italy. Expect long lines after midnight.
via libetta 13, telephone 065 748 272, open tue-sun 11pm-4am, metro garbatella

(V) A perennial favorite in Testaccio is **Akab**, although its popularity means long lines on most nights. This is a versatile place: some nights it's more of a pub/bar, some nights it's a full-on club (especially Thursday night when house music reigns), some nights it features film screenings and Saturdays are gay nights. If the line is too long, there are plenty of alternatives because all of the hippest clubs are along this street.
via monte testaccio 68, telphone 065 782 390, open daily 10.30pm-5am, metro piramide

(W) The **Supperclub** is a new way to eat out - a so-called 'dining experience'. Here you'll have all your senses titillated, from taste and smell to sight and hearing. If you go for the full dinner show, you'll be there from 9pm 'till 1.30am or so! You could opt to hang out in one of the chic salons instead for an aperitif, a late-night drink and a look at the art on display.
via dei nari, telephone 066 880 7207, www.supperclub.com, open 7pm-2am, price dinner (without drinks) €55, bus largo di torre argentina

Alphabetical index

Category index

transport

This guide has been compiled with the utmost care. Mo' Media bv cannot be held liable in the case of any inaccuracies within the text. Any remarks or comments should be directed to the following address.

mo' media, attn. 100% rome,
p.o. box 7028, 4800 ga, breda, the netherlands, e-mail info@momedia.nl

author	silke buhr
final editing	zahra sethna
photography	francesca pirzio biroli, rome
graphic design	www.studio100procent.nl, naarden
cartography	eurocartografie, hendrik-ido-ambacht
project guidance	joyce enthoven & sasja lagendijk, mo' media
printing office	south china printing co. (china)
100% rome	isbn 90 5767 115 8 - nur 510, 512
	© mo' media, breda, the netherlands, august 2003